THE RIVER RIBBLE

Overleaf: The tiny hamlet of Wharfe in Crumackdale. A stone over the doorway of the nearest
building bears an eighteenth-century date.

THE RIVER RIBBLE

by

RON FREETHY

TERENCE DALTON LIMITED
LAVENHAM . SUFFOLK
1988

Published by
TERENCE DALTON LIMITED

ISBN 0 86138 058 4

Text photoset in 10/12 pt Baskerville

Printed in Great Britain at
The Lavenham Press Limited, Lavenham, Suffolk

Contents

Preface and Acknowledgements

FROM its source in the limestone hills above Settle to its estuary between Lytham and Southport, the Ribble is one of the North's most beautiful and historic rivers. Neolithic people caught fish, hunted game in the once-dense forests and built forts on the breezy uplands. Roman galleys eased their way upstream to their settlements at Walton-le-Dale and Ribchester, Viking longboats carried fierce warriors to harass the Saxons. After one of their many battles a vast treasure was lost at Cuerdale, only to be discovered in the nineteenth century. The river and its tributaries provided the initial power for the industrial revolution. The grand old watercourse has survived all this and continues to delight the walker, naturalist and historian.

One problem with this book is brevity, as many facts have had to be omitted because of lack of space. This information has been gathered with the aid of a number of friends. I am grateful to Brian Lee, well known as a Ribblesdale aficionado, for his company and inspiration. To the librarian of Giggleswick school and to many other reference libraries, I express my thanks. To my wife Marlene I am grateful for typing and for a number of excellent photographs. To my son Paul I record my thanks for his eagle-eyed proof reading and attention to historical detail. Carole Pugh provided excellently drawn maps and lovely line drawings. Last but by no means least I freely acknowledge my debt to Elsie Baines who provided a constant stream of essential facts and invaluable comments. Without her this book would have been much the worse and I am delighted to dedicate this book to her.

Opposite: Scaleber Force, near Settle, where Stockdale Beck plunges sixty feet into a ravine—a scene which was much loved by the composer Sir Edward Elgar.

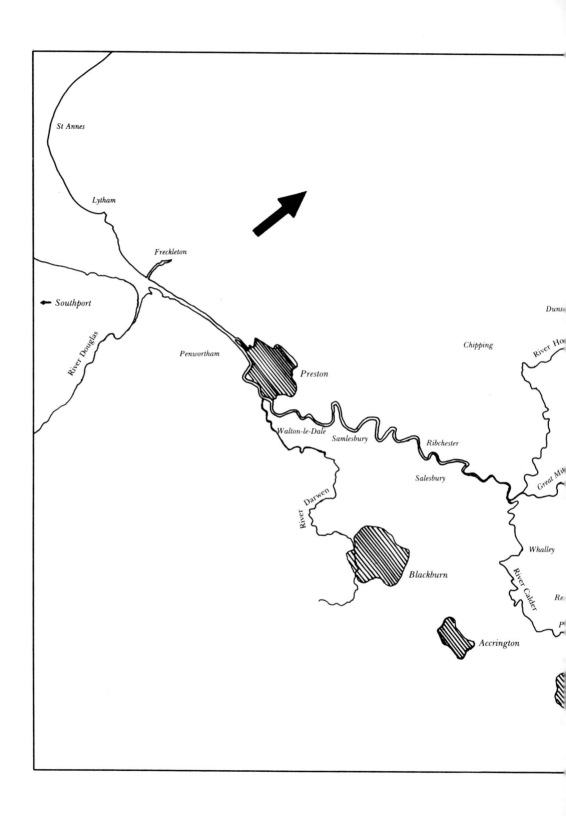

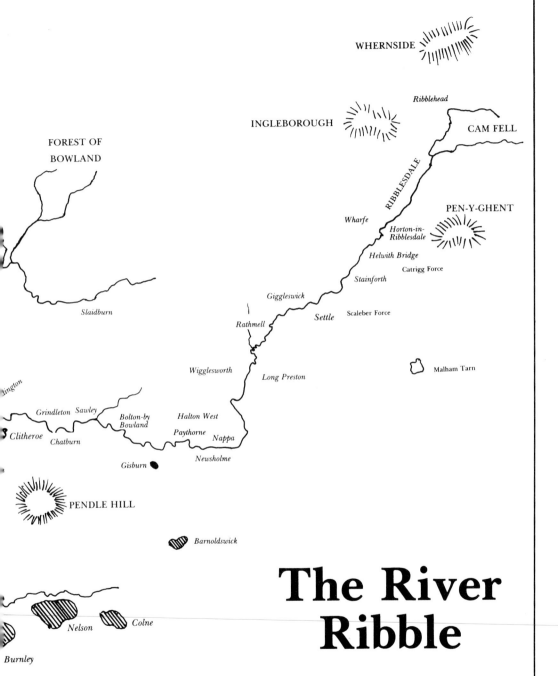

WHERNSIDE

Ribblehead

INGLEBOROUGH

CAM FELL

FOREST OF
BOWLAND

RIBBLESDALE

PEN-Y-GHENT

Wharfe

*Horton-in-
Ribblesdale*

Helwith Bridge

Catrigg Force

Stainforth

Giggleswick

Scaleber Force

Rathmell

Settle

Slaidburn

Malham Tarn

Wigglesworth

Long Preston

ington

Grindleton *Sawley*

*Bolton-by
Bowland*

Halton West

Clitheroe

Chatburn

Paythorne

Nappa

Gisburn

Newsholme

PENDLE HILL

Barnoldswick

Nelson   *Colne*

Burnley

The River
Ribble

CHAPTER ONE

In Search of the Source

I felt a strange excitement as I spent springtime in the Yorkshire Dales looking for a Lancashire river. The bubbling cry of the courting curlew mingled with the soaring song of the skylark and the fluttering song flight of the meadow pipit. The pink flush of dawn brushed over the tower of the church at Horton-in-Ribblesdale and as I followed the path towards the damp moors, water oozed from beneath my feet. A dry tuft of soft rush was the nest site of a snipe, the female sitting on her clutch of four eggs, while above her the male plunged out of the sky, producing the haunting sound which has been likened to the terrified bleating of a sheep, but called drumming. This sound is produced not vocally but mechanically by a pair of stiffened outer tail feathers, which are vibrated during the dive.

There were no other naturalists with me to share the dawning of the day, but below me were large numbers of folk easily divisible into three types, which I call steamers, joggers and potters. The steamers had gathered to wait for a grand old puffer train to pass along the Settle to Carlisle railway, so long under threat of closure but now saved, one hopes. The joggers were limbering up because this was the day of the three peaks foot race, and the potters were preparing to plunge into the bowels of the earth.

This is hill and pot hole country, but three peaks soar above the rest. Whernside is the highest at 2,419 feet (737 metres) its name derived from the word *quern*, an ideal description for a mountain with a cap of millstone grit. It was but a small step from using a stone for grinding corn to fashioning huge blocks into millstones driven round by the waters of the Ribble. The other two peaks are Ingleborough, which is 2,365 feet, (720.5 metres) and Penyghent, whose 2,273-foot (692.5 metres) peak can be reached from Horton-in-Ribblesdale.

I looked down at the water oozing from my boots, which squelched through the spongy mass of sphagnum moss, and wondered if here was

A curlew, bird of the marshy uplands, at its nest.
Bill Wilkinson

the source of the Ribble. Modern geographers would smile at my naivety, but stranger ideas were entertained in times past when few travellers ventured beyond Horton-in-Ribblesdale and thought mountains to be the homes of evil spirits and to be avoided at all costs. Perhaps the sound of the drumming snipe or the shadowy form of a hunting short-eared owl added to the apprehension; I have sometimes seen flashes of light arising from the boggy land as methane gas rising from the rotting vegetation spontaneously combusts. Will-o-the-wisps were always guaranteed to keep away all but the bravest or perhaps the most inquisitive souls.

Michael Drayton (1563–1631) the Elizabethan poet suggested as the source of the Ribble the very ground on which I was standing above Horton. In his poem *Polyolbion* he writes:

> From Penigent's proud foot as from my source I slide
> That mountain my proud sire, in height of all his pride
> Takes pleasure in my course as in his first born flood,
> And Ingleborough, too, of that Olympian brood
> With Pendle, of the north the highest hills that be
> Do wistly me behold, and are behold of me.

As a poet Drayton deserves our praise, but as a geographer he falls far short of the mark. There is no mention of Whernside being present at the birth of the baby Ribble; and by the time Horton-in-Ribblesdale is reached, and the river drains the slopes of Penyghent, it is almost adolescent. Pendle, situated some distance to the south, is, as we shall see later, below 2,000 feet and therefore smaller than any of the Ribble's three peaks. Drayton's contemporary William Camden (1551–1623) puts Ingleborough on the Ribble map pointing out (wrongly as it happens) that: "This river cometh with a quick and hasty stream out of the hills of Yorkshire taketh his first southward by three exceeding high mountains, Ingleborrow at the springhead".

This account at least suggests that the source is beyond Horton-in-Ribblesdale and gives some indication that the author may have been somewhere near the source. Leyland, writing in the early part of the seventeenth century, is extremely vague and mentions that: "Ribil riseth in Ribilsdale above Salley Abbey and so to Sally".

There is no arguing that this statement is true, the source of the Ribble being far beyond Salley, so this statement advanced knowledge not one jot. Although we are much nearer to agreement at the present time geographers are still not entirely in accord. Just beyond the hamlet of Selside two becks (*beck* is Norse for a stream) with their origins in the surrounding hills join forces at between 800 and 850 feet above sea level to produce the Ribble. These are the Cam and the Gayle, the latter being considerably longer; in consequence it is usually given the credit as being the source. I have listened to the old Dalesmen arguing in pubs all down the valley but most agree that to see the source the visitor must turn right at the T-junction of the Ingleton to Hawes road and proceed just beyond Gearstones. Once on the old cattle drove road from Scotland, the *Gearstones Inn*, now a private house, must have seen some high jinks in the old days when the Scots slaked their thirst. Their black cattle would have been hobbled and allowed to rest on the damp field below the inn. There was also a Wednesday corn market held at Gearstones as Dalesfolk stoked up in preparation for the snows, and especially the winds, which in these wild parts can paralyse a community. The corn market seems to have ceased about 1870 but the inn continued to operate until 1911.

Down in the dip below Gearstones is Gayle Beck. This scene must have been familiar to the Roman legions as they marched towards their small camp at Bainbridge. While researching this book I made three separate trips to Gayle, sometimes called Gale, Beck. The latter spelling

The Settle to Carlisle railway curves away across Ribblehead viaduct, with the station in the right foreground.

Hauled by one of Sir Nigel Gresley's famous A4 Pacifics, a train crosses the great viaduct at Ribblehead.

seemed to be most appropriate on the occasion of a November visit when an icy wind blasted down from the flat snow-clad top of Whernside. No use looking for wildlife on days such as this; I was quite happy to seek the shelter of the fire crackling in the hearth of the *Station Hotel* situated close to the T-junction and on the road to Ingleton. On the second occasion, just after Christmas, the temperature was down to −7°C but the clear blue sky allowed me to see for miles, and during a bracing walk over the frozen moorland I caught glimpses of a raven and a peregrine falcon. What a contrast to the middle of May when the day dawned clear and warm and red grouse called from the heather where they were feeding upon the succulent new shoots which make up the bulk of the adults' diet. "Go back–Go back" the males call as the hen sits tight on her eggs. On days like this they have no need of the feathering on their legs which cuts down heat loss in winter, enabling them to survive in the harshest conditions. The young grouse soon learn to appreciate the value of heather as food as well as for protective cover, but in the early stages they do require some body-building protein. This they find in the form of the

4

larvae of the daddy-long-legs (crane flies) and of the emperor moth caterpillar, a lovely green and yellow creature which also feeds on heather.

The other tributary in contention as the true source of the Ribble is the Cam, which arises from a series of several springs oozing from the soft bogs on Cam fell. As the water from one of these springs flows it has cut its way through the limestone to produce Ling (meaning heather) Gill. This is crossed by a sixteenth-century single-span packhorse bridge, which although repaired in 1766 has retained all its ancient characteristics. In some parts this tiny valley is so steep that even the sheep find it impossible to reach parts of it and this has allowed the preservation of such a wide variety of plants that the gill is a valued nature reserve.

All these Ribble springs are excellent spots to find plants such as butterwort, bog asphodel and soft rush, all of which were once important in the economy of the Dalesfolk in times past. Butterwort with its yellowish, rubbery-looking leaves and long-stalked purple flowers grows well by these exposed mountainous becks. In soils leached of nutrients it can supplement its nitrates by trapping flies on its sticky leaves and digesting their bodies after folding the leaves inwards to produce a sort of false stomach. The digestive enzymes are similar to those in the stomach of animals and which cause milk to turn sour. The plant was given its name of butterwort because it was used to sour milk to produce curds and whey prior to making butter and cheese. It was in great demand by country folk until superseded by commercially produced rennet. The roots of bog asphodel were used by the girls to produce a hair bleach. Soft rush grows well along the sources of the Ribble and if the long spear-like leaves are carefully peeled the soft white centre called the pith is revealed. The pith is rich in oils and will burn, especially if dipped in animal fat. Rush lighting was nowhere near as smoky or as weak as we often imagine in these days of highly efficient electric lighting. The old Dalesfolk did not, however, know the meaning of a power cut.

If we stand on the picnic site at the T-junction of the old Ingleton to Hawes turnpike with our back to Whernside and look down the Ribble valley we have Ingleborough on the right and Penyghent on the left. A string of fascinating settlements lies before us as we move slowly down towards the old town of Giggleswick on one side of the river and Settle on the other. Before we start the journey, however, we must look back over our shoulder at the magnificent railway viaduct which spans Batty Moss below Whernside. These days the Moss is the home of moorland birds but when the railway was under construction as many as 3,000 men and their families lived in conditions of the utmost squalor in a temporary navvy township called Batty Green. Between 1870 and 1876 this bleak moor was a hive of activity as clay deposited during the ice ages was ripped from the hillsides and fashioned into the 20,000 bricks needed each day to line the arches of the viaduct. Smoke spiralled up from the ten kilns and mingled with that from the blacksmith's forges servicing the regiments of horses which provided the essential muscle power. In addition to building the viaduct, which is one hundred feet high and supported by twenty-four arches, the tough workers also punched a 2,629-yard (2,403 metres) tunnel through the stubborn rock of Blea Moor. The whole seventy-two mile length of the Settle to Carlisle railway which also traversed the Eden Valley was a truly amazing feat of engineering and would almost be worth saving as a working museum, leaving aside its role as a vital communication line for the Dalesfolk. There is a much more practical reason for its preservation which was amply demonstrated in December, 1985, when floods severed the main Carlisle to London line and traffic was diverted through Settle, the only alternative route. It has also proved invaluable when derailments have closed the main route. During Easter, 1986, there were sixty-six trains using the route due to repairs between Preston and Lancaster and they made £1 million profit that year!

What a scene must have greeted the visitor to Batty Green in the 1870s. The blacksmiths hammering on metal, horses whinnying, the buzz of sawmills, the clanking of cranes mingling with the wind whistling through the rising arches of the viaduct which were seated down twenty-five feet (7.6 metres) through the soggy moss and into the bedrock. The wind has been known to blow so hard in this area that it has stopped trains on the viaduct and often keeps folk indoors for days on end. All this and the smell of cooking from the flimsy shanty huts in which families huddled to keep warm in the chill of a Ribblesdale winter. Strangely enough some of the huts had built-in fireplaces constructed of marble brought over the fells from nearby Dentdale. Many a fish pie must have been cooked over these fires; apparently the Ribble was almost denuded of fish, especially trout, as the navvies went on the hunt. There was unrestrained poaching as fish were taken in nets, grappled by hand, blown up with dynamite and poisoned with lime. In low water a favourite amusement on Sunday afternoon was to go down to the river armed with a huge sledge hammer. Every stone likely to shelter a trout was struck and the stunned or lifeless fish came to the surface.

There was also some culture in the form of a school, a hospital, an "unofficial" church and a library. Navvies worked a six-day week, but still found time to drink and fight. *The Gearstones* must have seen many a heavyweight brawl, and some navvies went even further. Perhaps the most criminal act was that of one George Young who threw a stick of dynamite on the inn fire, causing a great deal of damage to the building and its customers. This was, however, a minor health hazard compared to the ravages of smallpox which caused so many deaths that an unmarked mass grave was dug in the churchyard of St Leonard's at Chapel-le-Dale, which had to be enlarged for the purpose. This can still be seen as a hump to the right of the path leading to the tiny church, within which is a tablet commemorating those who died during the construction of the railway. There is another similar plaque down the dale in Settle church, but the few who could afford it had their own tombstones at Chapel-le-Dale.

Our journey down the Dale begins at Ribblehead, where many remnants of the old railway days can still be seen, including the battered old station. The waiting room once contained a small organ used in the church services which were conveniently held there. There is also a group of privately owned houses set away to the right and known as Salt Lake City, a reminder of the days when working Americans occupied the area. At one time there were settlements called Sebastopol, Jericho and

All signs of the navvy township of Batty Green have gone from around Ribblehead viaduct, which is one of the great engineering works on the Settle–Carlisle line.

7

the Garlic Huts. Beyond Salt Lake is a magnificent stretch of ash trees dominating Colt Park Wood which sprouts out of the clints and grykes of a limestone pavement. Sheep (and people) find the going tough on this sixteen-acre site, which like Ling Gill is botanically rich in consequence. The area is now administered by the Nature Conservancy Council, from whom a permit is required before visiting the site.

Colt Park was once owned by the monks of Furness Abbey and one must assume that the surrounding area was used as a stud, although the pastures away from the wood itself would have provided good feeding for sheep. In the wood grow a host of splendidly colourful plants including bird's eye primrose, mountain pansy, globe flower and the rare baneberry as well as orchids both common and rare. In the summer, buzzards are sometimes seen hovering on the thermals and the occasional peregrine causes panic among the small moorland birds including linnets, meadow pipits and the mountain blackbird or ring ouzel. This species is easily recognised by the white crescent around its throat and by the ringing call which echoes from the limestone outcrops.

Almost opposite Colt Park is Lodge Hall Farm, formerly Ingman Lodge, which was one of the granges of the monks of Furness. It retains its character despite alterations made in 1687 by Christopher Weather-

Some of the men who died while working on the seventy-two-mile line from Settle to Carlisle are buried in the churchyard at Chapel-le-Dale.

head, whose initials are seen carved over the door. Nearby is a Quaker burial ground; in 1696 John Moore, who lived at Ingham Lodge, was imprisoned in York Castle because of his refusal to pay tithes. Up in the breezy heights around Colt Park I always feel as if I am alone with nature, a feeling which would have been even stronger in the days before the railway came, when the highest occupied settlement in Ribblesdale was at Selside, which was so recorded by Normans who compiled Domesday.

The Norsemen had their "settlement by the river" which we translate as Selside (*Saether* meaning a *sheiling*, an enclosure for sheep), which was at one time also controlled from Furness Abbey. When the railway was built, the huge embankment required to support the line overpowered the village which has looked dark and hemmed in ever since. Until the turn of the twentieth century Selside used to throb with vibrant life every 24th June when it held its pot and cheese fair. The railway brought visitors, not only to Selside itself but to the nearby Alum Pot. This is one of the most famous pot holes in Britain, situated at 1,125 feet (343 metres) on the eastern contours of Simon's Fell, which is dotted with drumlins, long narrow mounds formed by the glacial drift. Alum Pot is to the west of the village, while to the east is Hull Pot and many smaller holes. It is impossible to think of this area of honeycombed limestone without pot holes and those who are prepared to risk life and limb to explore them. The experts come well prepared but there are others who take unnecessary risks, especially when rain threatens, and the cave rescue teams based around Settle are kept constantly on their toes.

The 198-foot (60.3 metres) deep Alum Pot was described thus by a Kendal clergyman, the Rev. John Hutton, in his book *A Tour of the Caves*, published as long ago as 1781.

> Another extensive subterranean passage slopes and winds by degrees until it enters the ghastly and tremendous Alum Pot. We went 157 yards along this "autre vast", till we came to a steep rock, fully 12 feet perpendicular, where we stopped: a wise consideration! We might have descended, perhaps, without danger, but the question was how were we to get up again, which, without ropes or a ladder, would be totally impracticable. At the far end was an elegant lofty dome, called by country people St Paul's. There is no doubt but if we had ventured further, we might have come to Alum Pot; at least, so near as either to have seen the water that stagnates at the bottom, or the light that is admitted into this gaping monster of nature.

The next recorded attempt to penetrate the pot—there were probably other non-publicised efforts in the intervening years—was in 1847 when John Birkbeck and William Metcalf, who lived at Weathercote House in Chapel-le-Dale, lowered themselves into the void. The party was well equipped and reached the passage known today as Long Churn. There are prettier stalactite formations in the Dales, but few can equal those in Alum Pot chamber for sheer size. When probed by flashlight the mighty cavern seems to be never ending and the chill of the atmosphere is increased by the continual sound of running and dripping water, including one tremendous cascade dropping almost sixty feet (18.3 metres). A group of geologists added a green dye called fluorescein to the underground watercourse to discover where it fed into the Ribble. They were surprised when it eventually appeared oozing out of Tarn Dub, which showed that it wound around on itself and actually passed beneath the Ribble, a distance of over two miles.

Not only do you find pot holers massing around Alum Pot but just downstream at Horton-in-Ribblesdale they mingle with fell walkers and naturalists gathering in the *Crown Inn* to discuss journeys about to begin or those just ended. At one time the village had two pubs, but the *Golden Lion* is now used as an outdoor pursuits centre; surely none can be more ideally situated. Nearby is a cafe, also popular with visitors. The word

A common sandpiper, a bird which is a familiar sight on the Ribble in summer. *Will Bown*

St Oswald's Church at Horton-in-Ribblesdale, with the bulk of Penyghent looming in the background.

Hortun means a settlement in a muddy field, a description which would originally have suited many Ribblesdale villages. In fact Horton appears to be two villages. At one end the *Crown* is surrounded by a cluster of cottages and the river is straddled by a twisting bridge from which a stile leads down to the stony bed of the Ribble. In the summer, larks soar over the daisy-patterned grass and common sandpipers enjoy their courtship flights over the surface of the water and under the arches of the bridge, their white rumps flashing in the sunlight. Around the inn and cottages screaming parties of swifts hawk insects, their wide bills held open to catch food on the wing.

At the other end of the village opposite the *Golden Lion* stands the church, dedicated to St Oswald, who was King of Northumbria in the seventh century. The building has stood for around 800 years, with Penyghent looming behind it. Close by, a Pennine Way footpath strikes upwards towards the mountain. One of Penyghent's foothills is called Plover Fell, which is thought to refer to the dotterel or small plover. This bird was once common but is now much restricted because of its trusting nature and pleasant-tasting flesh. On these high slopes the limestone outcrops are cushioned by mats of purple saxifrage, and in June cloudberries grow well on the summit.

Horton-in-Ribblesdale is referred to as Hortun in Domesday, but the church dates from the time of Henry I (1100–35) or perhaps to the early years of Stephen who succeeded him. The right to the benefits (called the advowson) was originally given to the monks of Jervaulx Abbey, and as we have already seen other parts of Ribblesdale provided income for the brethren of the distant Furness Abbey, while Fountains, Rievaulx and Salley, all Cistercian abbeys, also had extensive lands nearby. Christian charity had little part to play in the business interests of the Abbots, who functioned rather like local chieftains, and in the thirteenth century a great deal of squabbling took place over who owned what in Ribblesdale. By 1249 the advowson of Horton-in-Ribblesdale had passed via the Archbishop of York to the nuns of Clemmenthorpe, which was close enough to York to be kept under proper control. Quite a lot of the original Norman church remains, including some of the forty-one-foot (12.5 metres) tower, although most of the structure dates to the late fourteenth or early fifteenth century. The west window has some interesting pre-Reformation glass showing the coat of arms of Jervaulx Abbey, and also the head of Thomas à Becket complete with mitre. The parish records suggest that the plague was rampant here, as in the rest of West Yorkshire, between 1596 and 1598. The only plagues now are the hordes of tourists who head for the wide open spaces of Penyghent. Some take the time to look at the church, in which there is a brass dedicated to the memory of John Armistead. In 1725, he endowed the free grammar school, the remains of which are found near the churchyard. Modern scholars must make their way down the Dale to the high school at Settle.

"Whatever do their fathers do for a living?" a friend of mine once asked as she looked at a group of children playing in a field with a frisky pup. The main industry apart from farming is quarrying, evidence of which is obvious in this part of the Dale, although it remains surprisingly attractive. The modern workings are centred around Horton-in-Ribblesdale and Helwith Bridge, which is unique in that it spans the three Rs of rail, road and river. It is rather surprising to find that the settlement has no railway station despite the close vicinity of the quarries. A line did once run down to the track from the quarries, full bogeys running down by gravity and being pulled back by ponies when empty. Although the metal rails have long gone the old route can still be detected, especially when struck by the angled sunlight of early morning or dusted by a light covering of snow.

Helwith may derive from the old Norse words *hela* meaning a flat stone and *vao* meaning a ford, and thus we have a ford made with flat stones. Looking at the Ribble from Helwith it is possible to see that the river of long ago changed its course and once flowed westwards to join the Lune, but eventually erosion around Sherwood Brow resulted in the present course being followed.

Anyone interested in the pretty, almost "chocolate box" side of Ribblesdale should follow the Austwick road from Helwith Bridge and walk from the tiny hamlet of Wharfe up Crumackdale, which is dominated by slate and limestone, ensuring a rich tapestry of colourful flowers. Snails are also very common because there is plenty of calcium from which to make their shells. Song thrushes smash the shells on

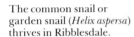
The common snail or garden snail (*Helix aspersa*) thrives in Ribblesdale.

stones; each bird seems to have its own anvil on which it hammers its prey to get at the soft body within. The word mollusc, the animal phylum to which snails belong, actually means "soft bodies". The visitor should find time to seek out the old houses, farms and barns. Stand on the clapper bridges with torrential hill streams tumbling and chattering beneath your feet. Enjoy the swallows flitting in and out of the barns and the dippers walking fearlessly into the headwaters, but never despise the industry which gives the area its economic viability. On our journey back to Horton-in-Ribblesdale let us look in on the quarries.

Arcow old quarry is now disused but is a Site of Special Scientific Interest (SSSI), mainly because of a fascinating geological feature known as an unconformity. At Arcow the younger, horizontal Carboniferous limestones stand unconformably on the eroded surface of steeply dipping Lower Paelaeozoic greywackes. The unconformity represents a time gap of several million years of missing geological succession. Devonian strata are almost totally absent.

The old quarry lies between the modern Arcow workings of Tarmac Roadstone and the Dry Rigg quarry of Redland Aggregates. These workings produce hard-wearing slates and greywacke. The latter is an anglicised form of the German *Grauwacke*, a term applied to sedimentary rocks laid down in the Palaeozoic period between 570 and 280 million years ago. It is a mixed detritus containing sandstone, feldspars and ferromagnesian minerals. It is this varying grain size which is the key to its value, for when laid on roads it prevents slipping. Whenever you drive on motorways or sit comfortably in an aircraft thundering along a runway you are very dependent upon Ribblesdale quarries, which are almost the sole supplier of this material. Out have gone the old quarrying methods and in has come computerised blasting and organised delivery. The folklore, however, lives on and old quarrymen have told me that they believe that an underground lake is trapped between the slate and the limestone; this explains why water often springs from the junction between the two. The slates were used locally for walls and roofing, although the quality has never been good. Once the railway came and Welsh slate became available the demand for local material declined. Other quarries produce limestone, and just how important limeburning used to be can be seen from the vast numbers of old lime kilns dotted about the area. It seems that each farm had its own kiln, but mass production was attempted.

Downstream from Helwith Bridge is Stainforth, and just beyond the bridge on the road to Langcliffe is an unusual lime kiln, visible from the road but reached by following signs to a waste disposal dump near the old

Left: An unconformity in Arcow old quarry, with the carboniferous limestone above the tilted greywackes.

B. H. Lee

Opposite: A primitive footbridge in Crumackdale not far from the hamlet of Wharfe.

quarry from which the limestone was blasted. This is a Hoffman kiln, a circular brick structure built to a German design. It is 150 feet (45.7 metres) around with sixteen separate burning chambers which the stoker could reach by walking around in a circle. "Artificial" chemicals have reduced the demand for "farm lime" but its industrial uses are many and the limestone quarries of Ribblesdale are kept busy. Blast furnaces need lime, as do paper mills and the tanning and building industries. The demand for whitewash has declined but the paint industry still requires lime, and so do sugar refineries and glassworks.

Between the kiln and Helwith Bridge is Stainforth, overlooked by the magnificent limestone hump of Winskill with its interesting assortment of erratics brought down by the glaciers at the end of the ice ages. Strictly speaking there are two Stainforths, split by river, rail and road. The settlements were originally called Knights Stainford (now Little Stainforth) and Friars Stainford (now the much larger Stainforth). The old name literally means a stony ford, and although modern Stainforth does have a bridge its most attractive feature is still the line of stepping stones across the rock-strewn Cowside Beck which drains Malham Moor. On its way to meet the Ribble the beck tumbles sixty feet (18.3 metres) over the tree-fringed Catrigg Force, a name suggesting that wild cats once lurked hereabouts. The friars associated with the old name were the monks from Salley Abbey, already mentioned.

On the opposite bank of the river is Little Stainforth, with Knights Stainford Hall which originally belonged to the Tempest family and then to the D'Arcys. In 1547 the hall was bought by the Watson family. Samuel

Watson rebuilt the hall and also provided a packhorse bridge over the river in the 1670s and this has been owned by the National Trust since 1931. Although the bridge has been repaired several times, none of the old features have been lost, and it is a fine example of the packhorse design as it is very narrow and has very low parapets. The horses were led in single file over the single span with their packs hanging over either side of the bridge. Samuel Watson was a Quaker who suffered imprisonment for his faith. He attempted to express his views further down the Dale, and while speaking at the "steeple house" at Giggleswick he was dragged down and had his head banged against the seats before being thrown out on to the ice. Samuel Watson did not give up easily, however, and on 30th May, 1688, the churchwardens at Giggleswick were told to "Go into him with all your might and we shall see that you are well backed up."

Below the Knights Stainforth packhorse bridge the Ribble cascades over a series of stony shelves, and then falls headlong as a mist of spray into a dark, deep pool overhung with trees and ferns which provide shade for trout and salmon. I visited the spot in late December, 1985, to find the limestone overhangs draped with icicles which looked just like the organ pipes of a massive cathedral organ. A caravan site run from the hall, which is now a farm, is busy in the summer but the visitors are easily swallowed into the silence of the rolling countryside. It is said by some historians that the bridge lies on the route of an ancient track which forded the Wharfe at Grassington, crossed Malham Moor, passed through the Stainfords and thence onward to Clapham. Here was the shortest possible route from York to Lancaster. What great events took place here, I wonder, when the knights of the Tempest family chose to fight for white against red in the Wars of the Roses?

Those with a taste for ancient history should move further down the Dale to Langcliffe, which means the "long cliff", and follow the path from the village past the Clay Pits plantation and then along a twisting path across fields and over walls to the scars and Victoria cave, discovered not long after the great queen's coronation by four lads out with their dogs. All of us who walk the countryside have seen gangs of youths with terriers, ferrets and larger dogs of the greyhound stock scouring the moors for "game". It was much the same in 1838 when a lad called Michael Horner and two friends from Langcliffe set off hunting and met

Catrigg Force, where the Cowside Beck drops sixty feet over a sheer rockface.

up with John Jennings, who had walked with his two terriers from his home in Settle. The dogs had already torn a hedgehog to pieces and were keen to try for larger game. They decided to try an area which they aptly named Foxholes. To their surprise the dog which they pushed into one hole soon emerged from another further up. The following week the group returned and in went Michael Horner, the first man to enter the cave since Romano-British times.

Since the discovery was reported by the lads the entrance has been enlarged; it is now nearly forty feet (12.2 metres) high and one hundred feet (30.5 metres) wide. Beneath this ancient midden layer after layer of artefacts and bones have been unearthed. Victoria cave has provided a wealth of material, some of which is on view in the Museum of Craven Life in Settle. The remains of Neolithic man were identified and also bones and skulls of reindeer, brown bear and even a fine skull of a huge grizzly bear. At very low levels bones of rhinoceros and hippopotamus were removed, along with those of the straight-tusked elephant, hyena and the wild ox, which was probably the ancestor of our present-day

Victoria Cave, which was the home of Neolithic man and has produced evidence of more recent occupation in the form of Romano-British brooches and coins.

The old packhorse bridge at Stainforth, one of many such bridges which survive in Ribblesdale, is said to be on an ancient track from York to Lancaster.

cattle. Remains of modern animals, including the badger, have also been found. Romano-British valuables, including silver and bronze brooches as well as coins, led to early over-exploitation of the site and some damage to delicate material may well have occurred. Fish harpoons with skilfully wrought reversed barbs found at many levels suggest that the Ribble was a reliable fishery.

Langcliffe, one of the few villages in upper Ribblesdale to be mentioned in Domesday, eventually formed part of the property which one Elias of Giggleswick gave to Salley Abbey. Domesday records that a notable called "Fech" was in possession of three carucates of land which were taxable. A carucate was a rather inaccurate unit of land defined as the area which could be tilled by one plough and eight oxen in a year. After the destruction of the medieval village by the Scots in 1318, it was replaced by the present settlement in a slightly different location about half a mile to the south.

The middle row of the present village, sometimes known as Cross

Houses in Langcliffe, one of the few villages in upper Ribblesdale to have been mentioned in the Domesday Book.

Green, once had an inn under the sign of a naked woman; the sign is embedded in the wall. There is a *Naked Man* in Settle, now not an inn but a café, and the two figures have a folklore surrounding them which is rightly looked upon by some historians with suspicion. It is said that the pair may have been part of some ancient nature-based religion replaced in the dim and distant past by Christianity. Did they come from the old village of Langcliffe? Until the historians come up with a better answer they should not cast stones at those who perpetuate the myth.

The doorway of the magnificently proportioned Langcliffe Hall is dated 1602, but the building is certainly not that old and the stone probably formed part of an earlier structure. There may even have been a third manor house on the site, from which two brothers of the Paley family left the quiet of Langcliffe to fight at Flodden Field in 1513. The most important family to dwell in the present hall, probably built by Henry Somerscales, were the Dawsons.

Isaac Newton (1642–1727) sometimes stayed at Langcliffe and it is thought that William Dawson was one of the first to read and understand the great man's *Principia*. Geoffrey Dawson during his periods of editorship of *The Times* from 1912 to 1919 and again from 1922 to 1941 often stayed with his aunt at Langcliffe Hall, and despite his eminence he failed to persuade the old lady to install a telephone. Important messages were sent to Settle station and a runner then carried them to Mr Dawson.

One institution which was lacking in the old village was a church and the journey down the Dale to Giggleswick had to be made whatever the weather. In 1851 a church was built in Langcliffe, and many a villager must have resorted to prayer in the period up to 1858 when there was a slump in trade and the cotton mills which had been converted from old corn mills stood idle. But it was a Wesleyan, Lorenzo Christie, who brought prosperity back to Langcliffe, and he was obliged to bring in extra workers from as far afield as Cornwall to meet demand, so the village was vibrant once more. I often sit on the circular bench surrounding an ancient tree in the centre of the village and listen to the splashing waters of the fountain in front of the post office. I look at the stout cottages and imagine my ancestors among the newly arrived Cornish workers looking out of their front door. They must have had to contend with winter winds driving a sheet of freezing rain down the valley as they scurried down to the mill on the banks of the Ribble. There was always the compensation of a regular, if small, wage packet, and the summer mornings with the sweet smell of crushed grass beneath the feet must have made winter seem far away. On Sundays they would go to the chapel while the "posh" went to the new church. When Hector Christie took over the business his strict Anglicanism led him to insist that his workers regularly attended the church rather than the chapel. He also provided a stained glass window, which was inserted in 1868.

One of the old mills is still being used, although only as a paper store. This was built in 1868, but there was another mill, now vanished, built by the monks of Furness higher up the river. The weirs and dams are also still present and here bird watchers, especially in winter, can watch wildfowl including tufted ducks, pochard, the ubiquitous mallard and the rarer, but increasingly common, goosander. The latter are saw-billed ducks; their long slim beaks have edges which are serrated, each "tooth" sloping backwards. This is an ideal mechanism for gripping fish, for the more they struggle the firmer they are held. Male goosanders have a green head with a great deal of white on the body, while the ducks have red heads and brownish bodies. These mills and also those downstream at Settle prevented salmon from reaching their breeding grounds, and reduced the Ribble fisheries to very low levels. The problem seems to have been that the Salmon Fishery Act of 1865 worked only if a river flowed for the whole of its length in one county. The Lancashire Justices dealt with the Ribble as a salmon river; the West Riding Justices disregarded that aspect, and looked upon it chiefly as a source of power for the mills at Settle.

A footpath runs from the mills towards Giggleswick and Settle via an attractive cluster of houses making up Stackhouse, which is dominated by the hall, dated 1695, the home of the Carr family. Their coat of arms, including three cocks, can be seen over the doorway. Before the Carrs the Brayshaws owned the surrounding lands but it was the former family who had most influence on the district. They were great benefactors of Furness Abbey and it was John Carr who was partially instrumental in the foundation of Giggleswick school. Around 1860 William Carr wrote an authoritative account of Shorthorns and was an acknowledged authority on breeding cattle, which must have thrived on the lush grass of the Ribble water meadows. At this time the market at Settle must have seen many a fine beast brought in for sale.

Icicles hanging from the limestone overhangs at Stainforth.

CHAPTER TWO

Settle and Giggleswick to Gisburn

SETTLE is a delightfully rumbustious spot and the commercial hub of the twin township with Giggleswick, less touched by big business, occupying the opposite bank of the Ribble. Settle only superseded Giggleswick when the railway arrived and cotton mills dependent upon cheap transport sprang up. The parish church dates from 1838 and is almost suffocated beneath the towering arches of a viaduct. Within the church is a marble plaque commemorating those who perished while the railway was under construction. In the Domesday record of 1080 "Setel, three carucates to be taxed" warrants only a brief entry and Stainforth, Langcliffe, Stackhouse and Giggleswick are all mentioned.

If you wish to see Settle at its bustling best then visit the Tuesday market, which was first granted at the request of Henry Percy in 1249. Avoid Wednesday, which is early closing. One side of the square is graced by the Shambles, one-time slaughter house of the town in the days when the market shoppers were less squeamish than we are today. It seems that the basements housed blacksmith's forges, store rooms and workshops, and over these the butchers carried out their bloody business. Initially the third storey did not exist and the general appearance must have been rather like a row of terraced houses with every inch of space intelligently used. It was the Victorians who added the third storey and for once seem to have enchanced the character of the building. Opposite the shambles is the mate of the *Naked Lady* to whom we were introduced at Langcliffe. Once an inn, the *Naked Man* is now a well-used café, one of many in a town which caters wonderfully well for travellers. Settle square has seen its share of controversy, not least during the time around the middle of the seventeenth century when George Fox's followers were beginning to challenge the established Church. The first Quaker preacher to visit Settle was William Dewsbury, who was born at Pocklington in the East Riding. He preached first at Sedburgh, where he was badly beaten, and then at Settle, where he fared little better. His words cannot have fallen on deaf ears because a Friends' meeting house was built at Settle in 1678.

There is no castle in Settle but it does give the impression of a fortified town due to the mighty crag of Castleburg which seems to hang, like a geological sword of Damocles, over the town. At one time there was the risk of rocks falling into the town around the area occupied by the Zion church, but the crag has been stabilised and a lovely walk leads from the town up to the treelined crag, from which there are magnificent views of the river. Eighteenth-century visitors did not appear to be quite so impressed and Thomas Pennant who came in 1773 thought it to be "a small town in a little vale resembling a shabby French town with a 'place' in the middle". The poet Thomas Gray (1716–71) was probably fairer in his assessment in writing that Settle "is a small market-town standing directly under a rocky fell; there are not above a dozen good-looking houses and the rest are old and low with little wooden porticos in front."

The modern highway, opened as a turnpike in 1754, leads from Settle past the *Falcon Manor Hotel*, under the railway bridge built in the 1860s and on to Long Preston, with the water meadows which were once called Ings of Ribble down to the right. There were, however, two possible routes before the turnpike and both these are still easily navigable even by car, although best appreciated by the walker with the time to stop and stare. The lower route on the opposite side of the river led through Giggleswick, Rathmell, Wigglesworth and Paythorne and thence to Gisburn. This is the route we shall follow in this chapter, but

The Market Place at Settle, with the Shambles where the town's butchers once slaughtered animals and sold the meat.

A wintry picture of
Stockdale Beck.

those who wish to see the best of Settle should take a return journey along the high road through the old town and on as far as Scaleber Force before retracing their steps.

The initial section is steep and winds upwards through the High Street to a fine-looking stone house with a date stone indicating 1679. From the outside it appears to be a rather magnificent old manor house. Why then should it be called Preston's Folly? Although there is a fine staircase inside, all the money was spent on the exterior and there was nothing left for the interior. An old farmer friend of mine once described an exclusive new housing estate, each "box" with a new car on the drive, as "a spot where the curtains is kept shut so that tha' can't see that they've only gitten jam and bread to eat". Preston's Folly, which now houses an antique shop, would seem to have been a seventeenth-century attempt to live up to the Joneses. The road twists and turns up from the Folly and passes little groups of seventeenth- and eighteenth-century cottages, many of which share a common courtyard. These could be sealed off to protect the occupants from the invading Scots. Similar yards are found in Kendal and other border towns on the military route to and from the North.

Once the houses of Settle are left behind the upland road assumes a wild attraction which is apparent throughout the year, but one walk through the January snow will remain in my mind for ever. A cold wind kept the snow crisp and the bright sun reflected from the ice crystals. The point at which Stockdale Lane meets the road to Kirkby Malham is close to the site of a supposed Roman encampment, although the traces are not apparent today. The Romano-British artefacts found in Victoria Cave do, however, show that the invaders had penetrated into these parts and we should never forget that the Romans occupied Britain for the best part of four centuries.

In the valley cut by Stockdale Beck close to where it is crossed by a stone bridge is Scaleber Force. The sixty-foot high (18.3 metres) falls are

Scaleber Force, a scene beloved of Sir Edward Elgar.

viewed best after a difficult scramble down through a steep ravine fringed by beech, oak, ash and sycamore. It is well worth the effort to reach the valley floor and walk upstream to stand beneath the Force, a very descriptive Scandinavian word for a waterfall. Once it has started to tumble into the abyss Stockdale Beck changes its name to Scaleber Beck, which goes chattering on its way over a stony bed towards the Long Preston road. This scene was one beloved by the composer Elgar, and I once spent a happy hour with a long-haired musician who had come to Scaleber early one morning to play some Elgar on his violin in a spot which might have inspired the composer. The walk to Long Preston from Scaleber is an old drove road called Edge Lane, but the historian will find more points of interest on the low road, and so we will retrace our steps back through Settle to the fascinating village of Giggleswick.

Giggleswick

In the first chapter we saw how Drayton's 1612 account of the Ribble's sources was somewhat wide of the mark, but the Ebbing and Flowing Well which he describes here:

> At Giggleswick where I a fountain can you show,
> That eight times in a day is said to ebb and flow,
> Who sometimes was a nymph . . .

is there for all to see, although lucky the person who sees it working. The knowledge, or perhaps fear, of the well was there in pre-Christian times when it was thought that a desirable wood nymph was being chased by a lecherous satyr. To escape him she assumed the form of a clear spring whose waters rising and falling were merely her heaving bosom recovering from the chase. The well is situated on Buckhaw Brow, close to the present main road from Settle to Ingleton, and was probably the one referred to by Isaak Walton in *The Compleat Angler* as a "well near Kirkby in Westmorland which ebbs and flows several times a day". The Kirkby referred to is Kirkby Lonsdale, which lies beyond Ingleton.

There are some lovely stories told about folk stopping to quench their thirst at the well without knowing of its ebbing and flowing qualities. One such tells of a horseman who watched his steed plunge its head into the well just at the moment that it began to ebb. Seeing his horse apparently drinking the well dry he imagined the animal was sick; he urged the beast gently down the hill and in a hushed voice told the ostler at the *Lion Inn* to wrap the beast up in blankets before it passed away from drinking too much cold water. Just above the well is Nevison's Nick, which was apparently named after a highwayman whose horse was so well refreshed after a drink from the well that it could not be caught. It seems, according to the diary of William Lodge Paley (1785–1847), the headmaster of Giggleswick National School, that the locals tended to add their own strength to the spring water. His entry for Easter Sunday, 1826, reads "Parents let their children go to the Ebbs and Flows to suck Spanish juice and water. Others more vitiated take liquor, and those children will doubtless do so when they got older, so these rediculous and sinful customs get perpetuated". Although the well was never "dressed" after the style of the Derbyshire wells there was certainly an Easter tradition which was carried on into the 1920s when hundreds made the pilgrimage. In times past the Ebbing and Flowing may have been more reliable, as it seems that quarrying the limestone on Giggleswick Scar may have disturbed the feeder streams to the well. Just what caused the ebb and flow began to occupy the scientific mind and in his *Rambles by the Ribble* (published 1877) William Dobson mentions that "The cause of the phenomenon long puzzled the philosophical world but the late Mr Thomas Hargreaves, of Settle, some years ago accounted for it on the principle of the double syphon. A model constructed by him to explain the operation of the well is in the Settle Mechanics Institution". George Birkbeck, who initiated the Mechanics Institutes and Birkbeck College, London, was a native of Giggleswick.

The best way to appreciate the respective positions of Settle and Giggleswick is from Giggleswick Scar, a limestone outcrop covered in trees, including some twisted old yews. The Scar can be reached from Feizor, or after a breathtaking climb from Stackhouse. From the top it can be seen that the old road did not follow the present A65, which loops around Giggleswick, but actually wound its way through the narrow village street past the church and on towards Clapham and Ingleton. Much of the land lies in a deep hollow marking the old boundaries of Giggleswick Tarn, which was only drained in 1830 and remained very swampy until 1863 when the land so created was finally cultivated. The small cotton mill which was sited at the outflow of the tarn could obviously no longer function, but the villagers are said to have lived for several weeks on a diet of eel pie, as the stranded fish were gathered by the bucketful. During the early days of cultivation a bronze age canoe eight feet long by two feet wide (2.4 by 0.6 metres) was found buried in the mud; it had been constructed from a single huge trunk of oak. This was removed to Leeds museum, where it was unfortunately destroyed during the bombing of the 1939–45 war.

The name Giggleswick has a Scandinavian root meaning the settlement (*wick*) of a chieftain named Gikel or perhaps Gigel. The village was in existence before Gigel made his wick, and the church is dedicated

St Alkelda's Church at Giggleswick, dedicated to a Saxon woman who was strangled for her Christian faith by Danes.

to St Alkelda, who was a Saxon Christian strangled for her faith by non-believing Danish women. Some historians have suggested that the name of the church may derive from the Old English *haeligkeld* which could refer to the Holy (Ebbing and Flowing) Well. I think that this is unlikely since the church at Middleham in Wensleydale, where the saint is said to have been killed, is also dedicated to St Alkelda. The church was not mentioned in Domesday, but the village itself was, which probably means that the Saxon church was in ruins; its foundations might well lie beneath the present building, which is first mentioned during the time that Stephen ruled over England (1135–54).

A charter was originally acquired by William de Percy, Earl of Northumberland, who donated the profits to the Benedictine Priory of Finchdale. These were retained until the dissolution of this institution in 1538. The period between the installation in 1190 of the first recorded priest, who was called Laurentius, and the dissolution of the monasteries was anything but peaceful in these parts. The church suffered greatly in 1318 at the hands of the invading Scots, quite probably the same party which destroyed the old village of Langcliffe. There was also much heartache and disruption during the Wars of the Roses when feelings ran high in these parts since the Ribble formed the boundary between the two counties. The political allegiances ebbed and flowed almost as often as Giggleswick's well! During these troubled times the church's sanctuary must have been used many times. It was during the fifteenth century that the present tower was constructed, probably as much for defence as to the glory of God. If the south door of the church is closed a piece of timber called the invasion beam can clearly be seen set into the wall; this could be dropped into sockets and the building effectively sealed, with the villagers inside protected both physically and spiritually from the invading forces. They might well have had a splendid knight to protect them. An interesting discovery was made during alterations carried out

The present-day buildings of Giggleswick School, which owes its existence to the foundation by James Carr of a chantry school in the churchyard of St Alkelda's Church.

in the last century, when the tomb of Sir Richard Tempest of Stainforth was found to contain not only his own bones but the skull of his faithful war horse. This valiant gentleman was knighted on the battlefield at Wakefield in 1460 when the Yorkists gained a momentous victory.

It was the custom at this time for rich families to decorate a portion of the church or section of a chantry or chapel and to pay for a priest to say masses for their own souls and for those of their friends. At one time Giggleswick had three such chantries given by the Stainfords, Tempests and Carrs. It was the Carr family who were instrumental in the setting up of Giggleswick School. The splendid institution really began as a chantry school funded by James Carr, the original building being a small, two-storey cottage sited in the churchyard. The majority of chantry schools were suppressed at the same time as the abbeys, but for some reason Giggleswick survived.

John Nowell was both vicar and teacher in 1553, and it was he who negotiated the school's charter. It was established as a "Free Grammar School of King Edward VI . . . for the erudition and instruction of children and young men". The school has not looked back since and some excellent headmasters have guided its fortunes, none more surely than William Paley who was in charge from 1744 to 1798. During his fifty-four years in charge, the academic stature of the school blossomed and many university scholarships and fellowships were established. Other headmasters were builders in stone, and during the period of Dr G. A. Butterton (1846–59) the school was rebuilt on the house system. Past headmasters and benefactors were commemorated in the names of houses including Carr, Nowell, Shute and Paley, but Butterton modestly left himself out of the list. A great deal of building also took place during the headship of the Reverend George Style, and a more recent house bears the name of a well-to-do ex-pupil named Morrison who owned Malham Tarn House, where Charles Kingsley is reputed to have written *The Water Babies*. Anyone approaching Giggleswick cannot fail to notice Morrison's gift to the school in the form of a chapel, with its green copper dome towering ninety-eight feet (30 metres) above the playing fields. Jubilee Chapel, so named because the foundation stone was laid in Queen Victoria's Diamond Jubilee year (1897), is built in the form of a Latin cross. Giggleswick became prominent on a world-wide scale in 1927 because it was selected by the Astronomer Royal as the site for his observation of the total eclipse of the sun. Visibility here was excellent, although neighbouring places were less fortunate.

One of Ribblesdale's most delightful strolls is down from High Rigg past the chapel and then onward to Settle on the ancient highway from Clapham to Giggleswick, used before the A65 was constructed. The village is severed by a stream called the River Tems, which is spanned by tiny bridges giving the impression of a model village. Near to the church is the *Black Horse Inn*, and a gate connected it directly to the churchyard. The connection between church and inn was vital in the days when travelling long distances to worship was the rule rather than the exception. Religion and conflict seemed to go hand in hand during the sixteenth and seventeenth centuries and the Giggleswick area seems to have been very much at the forefront of events.

Rathmell is the first village out of Giggleswick on the lower road and where the first college to train Nonconformist ministers was set up by Richard Frankland. Richard was born on 1st November, 1630, and attended Giggleswick School from 1640 to 1648 when he entered Christ's College, Cambridge, as a minor pensioner. John Milton was an ex-student at the college, which had a reputation for puritanism. After graduating as an M.A. in 1655 Richard was ordained, and for a while held a professorship at Durham College which had been founded by Oliver Cromwell. Life must have looked rosy indeed for the lad from Ribblesdale, but then came the restoration of the monarchy. The minister had then to agree to "assent and consent" to the contents of the Book of Common Prayer, and if he failed to give such an undertaking before the Feast of St Barnabas, 1662, then his living should be forfeit. Two thousand ministers including Richard Frankland found themselves thrown out of their churches. Frankland was a brave man; he even went to London and tackled King Charles himself, but without the desired effect, although the King is supposed to have said "I will do what I can". Frankland owned property at Rathmell and he returned home to make a living in the only ways available to him. In 1670 he founded an Academy to train Nonconformist clergy. College Fold, as it is called, is still there, set at right angles to the street. This did not please the Church authorities, who excommunicated him, and Frankland moved to Nattland near Kendal (1674), Catton Hall, Kirkby Malham (1683), Dawson Fold near Kendal (1684), Hartbarrow near Cartmell Fell (1685), Attercliffe near Sheffield (1686) and then back to Rathmell for the period between 1689 and 1698. King William III quashed the excommunication order and Frankland was buried in Giggleswick Church in 1698. Frankland's College Fold was the first of its type to provide such a training, and provided a model for similar institutions set up after 1750, first at Manchester, then London and finally Oxford.

The tiny settlement of Rathmell is therefore famous throughout the Christian world. It also has a more bizarre story which emphasises that the hamlet is in fact part of Britain. The "Tommy Johnson" saga was related by William Dobson, who in his *Rambles by the Ribble* says it was known "throughout the district as 'Rathmell in England'." The story goes that once upon a time, when the hay was being gathered from the "Ings" or water meadows, a haymaker having partaken somewhat freely of "lowance", fell asleep on a haycock and was left in the hayfield by his companions. Heavy rains came on, the Ribble overflowed its banks and the haycock or "hub", as the inhabitants of Craven would call it, along with its sleeping occupant, was floated a mile or two down the river. The following morning, he was roused by a farmer from his perilous position, and was asked his name. "Tommy Jooanson" (Thomas Johnson) was the reply. "What, Tommy Jooanson a Ramill (of Rathmell)?" "Aye, Ramell a England," replied Tommy, who surveying the country, and seeing a broad lake occupying the valley instead of the familiar features of his Craven homestead, appeared to think he had been floated to some foreign land, an event not considered very desirable for an Englishman in those days when the French and English were deemed natural enemies. Ever since, the village has been styled, from Tommy's description of it, "Rathmell in England". I cannot, certainly, quote anything corroborative of the tale from Whitaker or Leland, or any other historian or topographer; I only give it as a veritable Craven legend;

> I cannot tell how the truth may be,
> I say the tale as 'twas said to me.

The nomenclature of various farms in this township is rather remarkable. One is called Israel, another is named Egypt, while a third is dubbed Rome, and letters sent by post, and even cart-boards, have borne the address in addition to the farmer's name of "Rome, near Rathmell, in England." A look at a modern map will show that these farms still exist, even a Far Rome farm, and that very little building has taken place in the intervening period. They all have one thing in common — the green rolling Ribblesdale country with the Ings flooded in winter. It may be that Tommy Johnson said that he came from the Ings-land, in which case the tale related above might well be true, and the lad would have sailed close to the village of Wigglesworth on his way downstream.

Wigglesworth

This quiet village has had two narrow escapes and might well have been overwhelmed by the noise of industry or the clamour of pleasure. The Settle Mining Company was established in 1868 to extract coal from Wigglesworth, and a trial shaft was sunk before the scheme was abandoned as uneconomic and the thousand £1 shares became worthless. Some optimists remained convinced of the presence of huge coal measures, but more cautious geologists have expressed doubts. If not industry, then what about becoming a spa town as a rival to Harrogate? Most of the watercourses around the village are pure and unpolluted, with the notable exception of Stinking Beck which oozes down from Tosside and is full of sulphur. Perhaps it contained too much sulphur, and another scheme came to nothing.

Much of Wigglesworth belonged to the monks of Salley Abbey, but the Hammerton family were also powerful in the area. They owned large areas of Craven from the twelfth century onwards and obtained lands at Wigglesworth on the marriage of Adam de Hammerton to the grand-daughter of local landowner Elia de Knoll. Other carefully arranged marriages increased lands and influence and Wigglesworth Hall, now a farm, was once surrounded by an extensive deer park. Some rebuilding went on in the period between 1700 and 1720, but a small barn with a pre-Reformation doorway was possibly a chapel associated with the monks. There is also a large barn with a kingpost roof which is 165 feet (50.2 metres) long, one of the largest in Britain.

Whatever happened to the Hammertons? It seems that they knew which side to support when it came to the marriage stakes but were a little less sure when it came to politics. When the Pilgrimage of Grace, about which a great deal more will be said later, erupted in opposition to the dissolution of the monasteries by Henry VIII, Sir Stephen Hammerton sided with the monks and was hanged as a result. His son Henry apparently died of grief and the family's influence died with him, although members of the family continued to live at Hellifield Tower, the fortified Pele tower beyond Long Preston. The decline of the Hammertons in this fashion must have been felt both at Wigglesworth and at Long Preston which lies on the opposite bank across Cow Bridge.

Long Preston

This was indeed a long straggling town which had a priest, as its name suggests. Today it is a strange but pleasing balance between an historic and an industrialised village. The Romans had a camp here, sited on a knoll overlooking the winding river below. The views were so commanding that it is not surprising that the Roman camp was replaced by Long Preston's fine old church dedicated to St Mary the Virgin.

The lower part of the tower is Norman, although the top part dates only from 1760, and in the Domesday Book the church is mentioned and three carucates of land are listed as taxable. During the reign of Stephen (1135–54) the area came into the hands of Walter de Amundeville, who gave the church profits to the priory of Cuthbert of Embeshy (Embsay) at

A fine laburnum tree in the village of Halton West, near where the Ribble begins to change its character.

some time before 1153, but by 1150 it had passed to Bolton Priory on the banks of the Wharfe. After the Dissolution, which began in 1536, the manor of Preston became part of the extensive holdings of Henry Percy, the mighty Earl of Northumberland. At this time Hellifield was included in Long Preston parish and the Hammerton family had their tomb in the church. A stone slab bears the inscription: "Pray for the souls of Laurence Hammerton, and Isabella his wife, of Richard his soldier son and Elizabeth his wife, of the parents and children and all benefactors of this chapel or chantry [founded in] 1445". There is also some grandiose seventeenth century woodwork, a Norman font and a Jacobean pulpit dated 1726. Outside is a sundial dated 1659.

There is a strange tale of the link between Long Preston and Preston, which both lie on the Ribble. At the time Bonnie Prince Charlie tried to claim the throne in 1745, the noise and clamour of an army so fascinated a forward lass named Peggy that she set off to Preston to see it all for herself. Her tale was told in a *History of Preston* published in 1822.

> It is well known at Long Preston, near Settle, in Yorkshire, that in the year 1745, a buxom, handsome young woman of that place, anxious to see the Pretender and his army, went to Preston in Lancashire, for that purpose, a distance of about thirty-eight miles and after gratifying her curiosity, and staying for some time in or near the rebel camp, returned to her native village. This became so much the subject of general conversation, that it was the occasion of producing a ballad, which obtained as much notoriety in Ribblesdale as the famous historical ballad of Chevy Chase. The gentleman who has furnished this anecdote says that he has frequently heard her sing the very song of which she herself was the subject, twenty-five years after the occurrence and she had then, though advanced in life, the remains of a handsome face and fine person, which had doubtless been impaired by time, and a strong propensity to indulge in spirituous liquors. The strain of
> "Long Preston Peggy to Proud Preston went,
> To see the bold rebels it was her intent."
> was seldom carolled from her lips till she had been treated with a half a dozen or more glasses of spirits.

A version of the ballad which I have in front of me reads:

> Long Preston Peg to Proud Preston went,
> To see the Scotch rebels it was her intent;
> A noble Scotch lord, as he passed by,
> On this Yorkshire damsel did soon case an eye.
>
> He called to his servants, which on him did wait,
> "Go down to yon girl who stands in the gate,
> That sings with a voice so soft and so sweet,
> And in my name do her lovingly greet."

Visitors passing through Long Preston will notice the old village green overlooked by the *Maypole* hotel. During the industrial revolution the green was covered with stone flags and the hotel was called *The Eagle*. Aspects of the old working village are not far to seek, although in the summer of 1881 a flash flood caused Long Preston Beck to rampage through the village and almost carried away a cotton mill and an older corn mill. The main income of the village came from cotton, especially the manufacture of calico.

The views over the meandering river down to the Ribble flats are particularly impressive in winter, when it is obvious that just after the ice ages here was a huge lake. Some draining took place in the 1800s, and, in the mud, bones of such creatures as hyena, elephant and bear were discovered. The fertile alluvial land is still damp enough to be a haven for waders, especially lapwings and redshanks, and swans and geese find the area attractive when flooded. There have been several suggestions that this area would be an ideal site for a reservoir, but so far efforts to turn back the clock to the time just after the ice ages have been resisted. It is interesting to look at the stone walls which divide the fields reclaimed from the old lake. Farmers still keep the peculiarly shaped stones with "cripple holes" to let the water through in times of flood and thus prevent the pressure from destroying the wall.

Long Preston to Gisburn

Beyond Wigglesworth and Long Preston is an equally impressive stretch of river pushing between the hamlets of Arnford, Halton West, Swinden, Nappa and Paythorne. Just before reaching Gisburne Park the waters of the Ribble are swelled by those of Stock Beck which flows from springs above Barnoldswick through Bracewell, with its fine old church, and onwards through Yarlside.

Just outside Long Preston on the A682 are the seventeenth-century almshouses established by John Knowles, while beyond these a very minor road leads down to the river at Arnford, which must have been an important crossing point on the green roads before bridges were built. At Arnford is arguably the first pair of semi-detached houses, probably built for two brothers around 1690 and complete with mullioned windows and

The majestic bridge at Halton West, with smaller arches to accommodate floodwater when the river is full in winter.

Paythorne Bridge, from which the Lancashire folk used to watch the salmon swimming upstream to their breeding grounds.

ornate staircases of oak. Further downstream is the lovely bridge at Halton West, surely as majestic as any spanning the Ribble. The scenery is now beginning to change from the austere gorges cut through limestone overlooked by mighty crags, and then the Ings-lands which followed. This change was noticed by Dobson when he came this way back in 1881: "At Halton the Ribble is well wooded, and the well timbered sloping banks add much to the beauty of the scenery which is of a softer and more pastoral character than anywhere above Settle."

This idyllic spot has changed little and the village of Halton West rests under a colourful cluster of spring and summer blossoms, including some bright yellow laburnums. Further downstream but on the opposite bank is Swinden Hall, probably an ancient clearing where herdsmen took their pigs into the forest to feed upon acorns and beech mast. The old pack horse route, which now passes beneath the railway, can still be traced up towards an attractive seventeenth-century, three-storeyed house with mullioned windows.

Beyond the hall the track leads up to Swinden Moor Head. The view from this elevated spot is so good that it is easy to see that it was a good choice for the bronze age settlers whose artefacts were found here during excavations made in 1945. Lanes hereabouts lead to Upper and Lower Paradise, which just goes to show that there are degrees of everything! From Swinden Moor Head the road leads down to Nappa, and beyond a dairy farm in the dip stepping stones cross the Ribble, marking the site of an old crossing, quite probably on an old drove route. On the opposite side to the farm a hollow in the hillside marks the place occupied by the pound, which in wet weather held the animals until the water level fell sufficiently to allow them to cross. My last visit to Nappa was made just after heavy rain, which seemed so much a feature of the summer of 1985,

38

and I could not see even the largest of the stepping stones. I did see a mink swimming strongly along the swirling water's edge. It isn't often that fishermen, farmers, gamekeepers and naturalists are in total agreement, but the mink is regarded by all as an undesirable alien. Introduced from North America as breeding stock for fur farms, the mink has been escaping since the 1920s, and the wild population was increased by deliberate release of animals during the last war when there was neither food for the animals nor a ready sale for the pelts. Being non-natives, mink have no natural predators and can play havoc with fish stocks, poultry, game and wildlife, especially breeding water birds including mallard, coot, moorhen and little grebes. Mink could also be a danger to the salmon spawning beds hereabouts.

Salmon are, however, much more likely to be seen downstream at Paythorne where a widened medieval bridge was once thronged with people from all over Lancashire who came to celebrate Salmon Sunday on the third week in November. They watched the salmon passing upstream to breed, but there seem to be fewer fish these days and the tradition is dying out. There is a strange-looking building close by the bridge which could be the remains of an old mill, and one can see what might be a part of the leet. I wonder if there was once a clack-mill here. A clack mill, an early type of watermill, consisted of a single small pair of stones turned by water.

The lanes around the bridge are a riot of blackthorn in the spring and the black-purple berries of autumn sloes look as if they have been lightly dusted with powder. A footpath follows the east bank of the river southwards to Castle Haugh, which is the remains of a Norman motte and bailey. The motte (hill) drops sheer to the river and the bailey (fenced courtyard) would certainly have been difficult to capture. According to the *Victoria County History* (1912) there may not have been a bailey but the motte itself, while only twenty-five feet (7.6 metres) high, had a commanding view and was also surrounded by a seven-foot (2.1 metres) ditch. It was close by this spot that on a lovely May day in 1971 I watched an osprey plunge into the river, catch a large fish (probably a trout) and carry it to a perch, where the majestic bird fed delicately, its feathers gleaming in the sunlight.

Marked on the map close by are the remains of Newsholme Hall, but this has now gone. There may have been a small Roman camp hereabouts, although the *Victoria County History of Yorkshire* referred to above makes no reference to it. The traveller along the Ribble to Gisburn cannot fail to be impressed by Gisburne Park which is lapped and occasionally washed by the river. Apparently Lord Ribblesdale refused to drop the "e" although both the village and the railway did.

CHAPTER THREE

Gisburn to Ribchester

EVERY naturalist has a number of red-letter days, and if he is very lucky one special day above all others. The village of Gisburn gave me one such day way back in 1969. I was returning from a summer holiday in Scotland, during which it had never stopped raining. As I drove down the hill from Long Preston into Gisburn it was still raining so heavily that the headlights hardly penetrated the sweeping torrents. Suddenly I was forced to brake; there in the middle of the road was a bitch otter and her cub, their pelts dripping with water and eyes shining as they were dazzled by headlights. I turned off the paralysing beam, and when I switched the lights back on the lovely animals had vanished into the grounds of Gisburne Park. I know that such a sighting will never occur again, but this does not prevent the adrenalin pumping through my bloodstream whenever I approach Gisburn, especially when it is raining.

I have a copy of a slim hardback book called *The Ribble Valley and District*, published at Euston Station in 1912 by the London Midland and Scottish Railway Company, and its description of Gisburn is almost as true today as it was then: "Gisburn itself is a typical one street village paved with cobbles, one side of the street being higher than the other. A noble rookery in the thick plantations overlooking the Clitheroe road adds attraction to the village. Being on the highroad between Skipton and Settle and Blackburn, an immense amount of wheeled traffic passes through in summer". Gisburn is still not by-passed and wheeled traffic thunders through day and night, winter and summer alike, and yet the village has a surprisingly tranquil though "lived-in" feel about it. This is very evident on Thursdays when farmers come to market, as they have done since Henry III granted its charter in 1260. The street echoes with the twang of the local speech. The pubs do brisk business all day, thanks to the market licence, and country life is seen at its best. The bleating of reluctant sheep and the fast talking of the auctioneer, perched on the top

Sheep are auctioned at Gisburn market, as they have been since a charter was granted by King Henry III in 1260.

of the pens selling the stock to the highest bidder, mingle with the whimpering of the collies waiting in the shooting-brakes for their new charges. Life is also hectic during Whitsuntide when Gisburn horse races are held and draw a goodly crowd to "watch t'nags jump o'ert sticks".

Gisburn was mentioned in Domesday, but only as being "waste", and it passed into the hands of William de Percy. The family with the greatest influence upon Gisburn, however, were the Listers, who can trace their ancestors to John Lister, the sixth son of King Edward II who ruled England from 1307 to 1327. In 1312 John married Isabel, daughter of John de Bolton, the bow bearer of Bowland, and Gisburn was her dowry. Their original home was at Arnolsbiggin, now Westby Hall Farm, described as "being in the township of Rimington", where the family spent three hundred years. The family tomb and hatchment may be seen at St Mary's church, which was founded about 1135, the lower half of the tower being obviously Norman while upper parts date to the fourteenth and early fifteenth century. There is also a rather puzzling monument to Sir John Assheton who died at his home at Whalley Abbey in 1697. Why, I wonder, was he not commemorated at Whalley?

At the end of the seventeenth century the Listers removed to what

was first called Lower Hall but is now Gisburne Hall. In 1797 Thomas Lister, the then head of the family, raised and equipped at his own expense a troop of yeomanry cavalry and trained them ready to meet the very real threat of a Napoleonic force invading Britain. For this patriotic act he was created Baron Ribblesdale. From an architectural point of view Gisburne Hall lacks elegance, yet few buildings have a more attractive site. It stands proudly on an eminence overlooking the substantial confluence of Stock Beck and the Ribble in the midst of a beautiful and richly wooded park. The railway slices through part of the park, although its passage was initially resisted by the Listers. Compromise was reached when the bridge design was altered to look like a castle and the line was sited so that it could not be seen from the hall. The 1912 railway guide notes "The summer house known as the temple overlooks the junction of the beck and the river. Up to the year 1880 this delightful place was open without let or hindrance to the public, but in consequence of the misbehaviour of a picnic party it has since been closed except to those having permission to pass within the gates . . . The public have access, however, to the Stockbeck road which passes through the estate and gives an excellent view of the hall."

Opposite: A quiet day in Gisburn, which on market days can be very busy indeed.

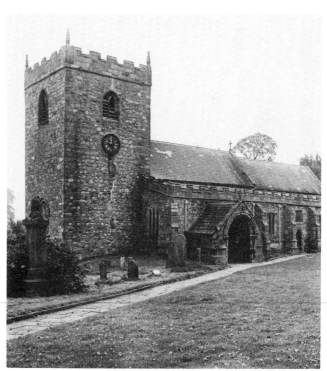

Right: St Mary's Church at Gisburn, founded about 1135 and still containing evidence of its Norman beginnings.

These views are still there although the Listers have now gone and their hall serves as a private hospital. It is difficult to imagine a better place in which to get well. No wild white cattle now roam in the park—they went in the early nineteenth century—one beast apparently being donated to the Manchester Museum. The cattle were apparently hornless and perfectly white, apart from their very black noses. They were brought to Gisburn from Whalley after the dissolution of the Abbey, and after they were removed from Gisburn the herd was maintained for a while in Lords Park below Clark Hill, but is now extinct.

The present-day naturalist, however, is often rewarded by sightings of both red and grey squirrels and of herons fishing in the watercourses. Hunting was very much part of the life of the Ribblesdales and both deer and otter were their quarry. In 1906 Lord Ribblesdale and a Mr Ormerod imported some animals from Ireland which were optimistically described as buck hounds. Contemporary accounts add no little confusion, since the dogs were described as "Kerry beagles", black and tan in colour and so much alike that they were difficult to distinguish individually. They were only around twenty-four inches (60 centimetres) tall, which seems a little small for hunting deer. It was admitted that only two or three couples had ever hunted deer, but all had hunted mountain hares in Kerry and preferred chasing rabbits and hares to deer. Even the term beagle is a little worrying, and one wonders if Mr Ormerod and Lord Ribblesdale were the victims of a confidence trick. The dogs were kept at Elanthorpe and to this day they have an impressive pack of hounds there which hunt the hare. While hunting might not be to everyone's taste, the dogs look and sound magnificent and are beautifully organised by the huntsman in his smart red coat. The smell of leather and warm horses also adds a feeling of nostalgia to many a winter's day. At one time the hounds were kennelled at nearby Bolton-by-Bowland, but they are now back in their original home at Elanthorpe. This would seem to be on the same site as the lost village of Haluuidetorp mentioned in Domesday Book.

Until the early 1970s, when the lovely creature was at last given protection, otter hunting was a regular occurrence along both the Ribble and the Hodder. The Wharfedale pack of hounds, which despite its name was kennelled at Giggleswick, was marshalled by the green-coated huntsman who hunted on foot and poked his long stick into likely looking holes among the roots of overhanging trees, especially alders. I often watched the hunt gathering at Gisburn Bridge, hoping that they would be unsuccessful and that none of the dogs would be hurt.

Close to the bridge is an old mill, built into the end of which are sculptured stones depicting the arms of the Percy family. These have

Hunting continues to be a part of the life in Ribblesdale: the Bolton-by-Bowland Hunt at its kennels.

obviously been removed from the ruins of Sawley Abbey further downstream. The views from the bridge, both up and down river, are magnificent, with oyster catchers, common sandpipers and grey wagtails finding the shingle beds much to their liking both as feeding and potential breeding sites. There are stretches of deep brown water where the mayflies emerge during a late spring evening from their aquatic pupal cases, only to be snapped up by the hungry trout. Small wonder anglers pay a high price to fish this stretch. The Ribble's banks are lofty, sloping and still richly wooded along the three-mile stretch leading down to Bolton-by-Bowland, through which passes Tosside Beck on its way to join the main river, having already absorbed the substantial Bond Beck.

Bolton-by-Bowland

On the road from Gisburn to Bolton-by-Bowland are two fine halls, one named Closes being described in 1905 as modern. The other—Fooden—is very much older and thought to be early seventeenth century. Now a farmhouse, the attractive building still retains its mullioned windows and the appearance of having been an important manor house. A 1905 issue of *The Rambler* magazine describes the scene thus:

> The pathway strikes between the house and the farm buildings, and then proceeds across the fields, only to emerge into the roadway again just at the top of the hill near Bolton-by-Bowland . . . One special feature of the place is the presence of a splendid mineral spring, a kind of little Harrogate . . . the water runs in a fair stream from beneath a ledge of rock, and leaves a deposit of sulphur all along its course. The stench of sulphuretted hydrogen—a kind of essence of rotten eggs—is keenly felt. Three or four glasses were borrowed from the adjacent farm, and the water, which is as clear as crystal, was sampled. Wry faces followed the test, in many instances, but we fancy that it was more rather from the smell than the taste. What can be done here in days to come we trow not, but the scenery and the waters combined ought to cure any ailment that flesh is heir to . . . we departed from the usual footpath, and made a journey to Denham Wheel. Here is a spot of great beauty. As we emerge on the banks of the Ribble, after having traversed the narrow path through the wood . . . we behold a beautiful natural weir, which runs in a diagonal direction across the river, and over which the water rushes in a silvery cascade, thence to fall into a very deep hole, in which the water is moved round, making a miniature whirlpool which accounts for the name of the place.

In fact wheel is an old Scandinavian word for a whirlpool and we shall meet it again at Salewheel, downstream of Ribchester.

The village was referred to as Bodetone in Domesday and then as Bolton-juxta-Bowland before assuming its present title of Bolton-by-Bowland, having had its market charter granted during the long reign of Edward III (1327–77). John de Pudsay was also granted free warren in the area, thus firmly establishing a family whose influence on the village was evident for centuries. Although their once-splendid hall has been demolished, the history of the family can be traced by visiting the church of St Peter and St Paul which dominates the space between the two village greens. Within the church is a memorial to Sir Ralph Pudsay, his three wives and twenty-five children! Sir Ralph was not only a supporter of the marriage stakes but was also a staunch supporter of Lancashire's red rose. He proved his loyalty by offering sanctuary to King Henry VI at

Pendle seen from Bolton-by-Bowland.

Houses bordering the Large Green at Bolton-by-Bowland, a village which had a market granted by charter in the reign of King Edward III.

Bolton Hall following his defeat at the battle of Hexham in 1464. In the grounds of the hall is Henry's Well, which local legend tells us that the King had dug and walled to serve as his private open-air bath. The Royal adventures in these parts did not have a happy ending as related in this chapter in the section on Brungerley.

The Pudsay family never seemed to be short of characters. It was towards the close of the sixteenth century that the extravagant William Pudsay annoyed Elizabeth I and made his famous leap. The whole story is something of a tangle, with truth and fiction firmly entwined. William was, as usual, short of hard cash and went out for a ride in order to do a little private thinking. While resting in a wood he met a gaggle of fairies who gave him a magic bit for his horse, which gave the beast extra strength. They also gave him the location of a vein of silver supposedly on the site of the Rimington lead mines but then called Skelhorn. Not all the story is fiction, because Pudsay did find silver and soon set up his own mint producing Pudsay shillings, which was illegal. Elizabeth's commissioners were on their way to arrest William when he grabbed his magic bit, saddled his horse and galloped off, escaping the law by jumping from a limestone cliff overlooking the Ribble, once known as Rainsber Scar and now Pudsay's Leap. He is supposed to have reached Elizabeth and pleaded his case, pointing out that it was ignorance and not forgery which had annoyed the Queen. In a sense he was correct, since the coins were not copied and the silver had not been clipped from existing coins. He had even engraved his own mark which was "an escallop" on the coins, some of which still exist in private and museum collections. The Queen pardoned William, who may have been her godson, but the Rimington complex was made a Mine Royal and the family were never allowed to make use of it again. All the profits went to the Crown.

After the Civil War the family sold the surrounding land. Eventually they ran out of male heirs and with the death of Bridget Pudsay in 1770 the line ended. In the twentieth century even their magnificent Bolton Hall was demolished, although a private road still passes through the grounds to the river and some evidence of the once superlative gardens can still be seen. Indeed, it has been suggested that Bowland gets its name from the bed in the river near the hall. The family will, nevertheless, live for ever in the name of Pudsay's Leap and because of the tombs and inscriptions within the church. A church certainly existed by the twelfth century but the present building dates mainly from the thirteenth, with the late fifteenth century tower its most attractive feature. There are few similar structures in Northern England and it is thought that it was being constructed while Henry VI was in hiding with Sir Ralph Pudsay. Because the tower has several features reminiscent of those in Somerset it is thought that the King, who knew that county well, had a hand in the design.

Sawley

I wonder if Henry ever walked the riverside path which leads to the village of Sawley and spoke with the Cistercian monks who had their abbey on the banks of the Ribble. Then known as Salley, meaning the "field of the willow trees", this abbey had a very chequered history and if its manner of living was mundane the same certainly cannot be said about its passing. When in 1147 the party of thirteen monks—an abbot and twelve followers to fit in with the concept of Jesus and his disciples—arrived on the wetlands after a journey from their mother house at Newminster in Northumberland, a hard task awaited them. The land given by William de Percy did not tame easily and the monastic crops often failed, and as late as 1187 there were thoughts of leaving Salley and trying again in a more favourable area. A look at the ruins shows the lack of wealth: the building materials were not the expensive ashlar of the richer abbeys but a mixture of black shale and boulder stones. Hard work and prayer worked wonders, and towards the close of the thirteenth century an impressive church 185 feet (56.4 metres) long towered over the Ribble and it seemed that the troubled times were over. Then came disaster in the form of a rival abbey built just downstream on the Calder, one of the Ribble's main tributaries. Whalley Abbey will be described more fully in Chapter Six. Suffice it to say at this point that the Cistercians who came to Whalley in 1296 had already failed to conquer a stretch of land on the banks of the River Mersey at Stanlow. No wonder the Salley monks were angry when these "failures" arrived to build a splendid abbey on a stretch of fertile land given them by Henry de Lacy. The new abbey meant that there were now two bidders in the local markets and the prices went up accordingly. This event halted the progress of Salley, and if it had not been for its brave fight against Henry VIII few folk would ever have heard of Salley. For so long enemies, Salley and Whalley stood together against the King.

The "Pilgrimage of Grace" as it has become known was really the North of England's response to the King's determination to dissolve the monasteries, break the control of the Pope in his realm and establish the Church of England with the monarch himself at its head. Henry's basic philosophy, engineered by Thomas Cromwell, was to prove that the smaller monasteries were corrupt and remove them on these grounds, hoping that the larger establishments would stand idly by. The King could then turn his attention to the larger monasteries and pick these off gradually.

In 1536 an arbitrary income of £200 per annum was decided upon and all establishments below this figure, which included both Salley and Whalley, were threatened with dissolution. Most surrendered peacefully enough and it must be admitted that the monks were then fairly treated, but led by a one-eyed Yorkshire lawyer named Robert Aske several northern abbeys resisted and the Rebellion of the North, otherwise known as the Pilgrimage of Grace, gathered momentum. It was not so much an armed conflict as a show of strength to try to convince the king of local opposition to his policy. Nevertheless Henry wrote to Lord Derby, his lieutenant in Lancashire, in fiery language on 28th October, 1536, ordering that "If on your coming to Salley, you find the abbot or monks or canons restored again, of which they must have been either authors or abettors, you shall at once cause the abbot and certain of the chief monks to be hanged on longpieces of timber or otherwise out of the steeple". These instructions would have come as something of a shock to Derby, as he must have been brought up close to monastic influence and was probably tutored by a monk. Although the Salley monks may have obeyed him, they seem to have returned to the abbey when he went away.

On 10th February, 1537, Henry discovered that Abbot William de Trafford was still master in his own house and fired off an unambiguous command to Derby pointing out that "You shall without pity . . . cause the monks to be tied up without further delay." The abbot, along with Paslew of Whalley (see Chapter Six) was taken to Lancaster, the rebellion was severely put down and the two monks were hanged, their abbeys at last united—but only in death. At one time an arch of monastic stone used to straddle the road, but motorists seemed to find it difficult to negotiate and it now guards only the entrance to a field.

The ruins of Sawley Abbey, or Salley Abbey as it was once known, whose monks resisted dissolution and suffered the consequences.

The main road through Grindleton, a village notorious for the fire-and-brimstone sect which took its name from the parish.

Just beyond this is the *Spread Eagle* hotel, overlooking the river at the point close to where the monks probably had a corn mill. In the eighteenth century this came into the hands of Sir Robert Peel's father, who converted it to a cotton mill; it now functions as a Wesleyan chapel. Remains of the old mill leet can still be seen. The graceful bridge which spans the Ribble has ancestors dating back to the reign of Edward 1, when Henry de Blackbrun paid two shillings per year towards its upkeep. The first bridge might well have been constructed by the monks, and the present structure bears the marks of ten masons. Across the bridge are attractive little cottages and a Quaker meeting house, and from both sides a series of footpaths ideal for walkers and naturalists leads through beautiful scenery. The village lies directly on the Ribble Way with walks leading to Pudsay's Leap in one direction and downstream to a string of fascinating villages in the other. Grindleton, Chatburn, West Bradford and Waddington all have their own individual charm.

Grindleton

The walk I took towards Grindleton along the river on a glorious spring evening was breathtaking. Pendle looked serene, and even the wisp of white smoke from the cement works at Horrocksford looked lovely against the blue of the sky. The bridge which spans the old Grindleford is architecturally unremarkable, but is a wonderful spot to stand and watch swallows hawking insects as they rise from the swirling deeps. The road from the bridge climbs into the village, passes the *Duke of York Inn* and goes on to the parish church of St Ambrose. Grindleton also had its own hydro at one time, now part of Riversmead school, and had both lime and sulphur springs, but it was Roger Brereley's fire and brimstone which brought fame—perhaps notoriety would be a better word—to the village. Brereley founded a religious sect that became known as the Grindletonians, which Frank Hird described as follows:

A curious sect called the "Breirlists" or "Grindletonians" was founded by Roger Brereley or Brierley, a clergyman, who was one of the Brereleys of Marland, near Castleton. For some years he was at Grindleton in Yorkshire, whence the sect took his name. But later he was perpetual curate of Burnely Church; he died at that place in 1627. During his time in Yorkshire, Brereley suffered much persecution, and at one time was a prisoner at York pending the hearing of fifty charges against him for false teaching. Not a single charge could be proved, and he was set at liberty. Brereley was a poet as well as a preacher, and his sermons and poems were published in 1677, under the following lengthy title: *A Bundle of Soul-convincing, Directing and Comforting Truths, clearly deduced from diverse Texts of Holy Scripture, and practically improven both for Conviction and Consolation: being a brief summary of several sermons preached at large by that faithful and pious Servant of Jesus Christ, Mr Rodger Breirly, Minister of the Gospel at Grindleton in Craven.* In the preface of the book we are told that Brereley's "life and conversation were comely in the eyes of the sons and daughters of Sion, and beautiful in the streets of that city, so that none could lay shame thereon." This gentleman of the "comely" life and conversation had some merit as a poet, as is shown by the ingenuity of the lines which conclude a poem called *Self Civil War:*

> "I can not with my self, as I conceive
> Wretch that I am, my self, my self deceive.
> Unto my self, I do my self betray,
> And from my self, banish my self away,
> My self agrees not with my self a jot,
> Knows not my self, I have my self forgot,
> Against my self I have mov'd wars unjust,
> I hurt myself and I my self distrust,
> My self I follow, and my self I fly,
> Besides my self and in my self am I.
> My self am not my self—another some
> Unlike my self and like my self I am,
> Self's son self furious and then wayward else
> I cannot live with nor without my self."

Looking through my diaries written over the last twenty years it is possible to pick out my favourite walks along the Ribble and the fact that I have almost fifty references to the gentle stroll from Grindleton to Chatburn speaks for itself. I have wandered among drifts of spring flowers including celandine, primrose and dog's mercury, photographed the white spring blossom of blackthorn and collected the sloes from its autumn branches and followed the tracks of a fox through deep drifts of snow. Close to the point where the river is bridged is a small sewage farm, which adds to the interest of the bird watcher. The decaying sewage is sprayed and aerated and as it decays (the smell is confined to a small area) it produces heat and this prevents the material from freezing. In the long freeze of February, 1986, the area was home to kingfishers, lapwings, redshanks, golden plovers and literally thousands of starlings, pied wagtails and black headed gulls.

Chatburn

Climbing the steep fields lined with hawthorn leads to the somewhat industrialised village dominated since 1838 by a church with a splendid looking tower, dedicated not to a saint but to Christ Himself. This is perhaps surprising because the village takes its name from St Chad or Ceatt who was one of the early bishops of Lichfield. There may well have been signs of life in the Chatburn area during Roman times as the military road from Ilkley to Ribchester sliced between Worston (see Chapter Four) and Chatburn. The road actually crossed Chatburn Beck, and a Roman presence was proved in 1788 when an urn was dug up containing a huge collection of silver *denarii*. Chatburn doubtless grew quickly during the early years of the industrial revolution, but its ancient religious roots can still be seen by reading the street names. Chapel Croft

Opposite: St Ambrose's Church at Grindleton in its pleasant setting.

Right: Chatburn Church with its spire.

indicates the one time site of the ancient chapel of St Martin which was destroyed by the Parliamentarians at the time of the Civil War.

Despite its industry Chatburn has retained an historic charm, and its long-established corner shop, once a toll house, selling Hudson's ice cream still draws cyclists and motorists, many of whom—the present writer included—are following in their parents' footsteps. During the last war a damaged German aircraft jettisoned a land mine which hit a tanker and just missed the mill. It did, however, damage a row of cottages and one woman was killed.

Cotton was for a long time the village paymaster, but while one mill continues to operate, the modern scene is dominated by the massive

Crinoid stems in carboniferous knoll limestone from a quarry at Twiston.

cement works. Long, long before the advent of the destructive human species, this area was swamped beneath a warm coral sea, and as it shallowed and finally disappeared the bodies of the marine animals became sedimented into limestone reefs. These tend to support a rich population of flowers. Many reefs have already been quarried to provide building and road stone, and particularly to satisfy the modern world's insatiable appetite for cement. In 1825 six lime masters were busy in the Pimlico area, ten kilns burned an average of forty weeks each year and "lime roads" led out of the Clitheroe area to all parts of the county and beyond. The packhorses would return with coal and slate. It is often said that old Clitheroe was noted for Lime, Law and Latin. One worked-out quarry to have become famous is Salthill, which since October, 1982, has had a geological trail; fascinating fossils including crinoids, syringopora and emmonsia abound. Only Horrocksford quarry is still working; Ribblesdale Cement lorries still thunder along roads lined with trees white with lime dust. Opposite the main works lies the charming village of West Bradford and from it footpaths run on both sides of the river down to Brungerley.

West Bradford to Brungerley, Waddow and Waddington

West Bradford is a village of contrasts, with quaint old cottages mingling with modern commuter housing. Some of the older properties are reached by crossing small stone bridges across a narrow stream which leads down to the Ribble. There is also an old cotton mill, a sign that West Bradford flirted, but not seriously, with industry. It did, however, play host to the world statesman Mahatma Gandhi, who stayed with Percy Davies at Heys Farm from 21st to 23rd September, 1931. He was on a fact-finding tour of Lancashire's cotton mills at Darwen and Blackburn which exported to India.

There is a spectacular circular walk linking the two plain bridges at West Bradford and Brungerley. There can be few places along the banks of the Ribble which can have witnessed more action than the area now spanned by the bridge at Brungerley. During the turbulent times of the

Peaceful enough today, Brungerley Bridge lies in an area which has known historic upheavals and popular excursions.

Wars of the Roses King Henry VI, as we have seen, fell upon hard times and was obliged to seek shelter in the houses of his supporters. The Tempest family were friendly and after his stay at Bolton-by-Bowland the King stayed at their hall at Waddington. The Talbots, another prominent local family, were devotees of the Yorkist King Edward IV, and when they discovered the Lancastrian's whereabouts the hunt was on, and he had to flee in the middle of his dinner. In the days before the bridge was constructed at Brungerley the Ribble was crossed by stepping or hipping stones, and it was while crossing these that Henry was captured. He was then taken to London, and if legend is to be believed he had to make the journey tied to the stirrups of his horse and facing towards its tail. He must have been a tough fellow to survive this journey.

It is now a popular and often quiet walk, with naturalists on the lookout for the white butterbur *Petasites alba*, a rather rare plant. There have, however, been times in the past when Brungerley looked more like Blackpool on a bank holiday, a scene graphically described in a magazine called *The Rambler* in May, 1906, when visitors were invited to:

> descend the somewhat tortuous and slippery path, which leads out into the open glade at the well known boating establishment of Brungerley Bridge. This was established some years ago by Mr Eli Tucker who occupied Brungerley for a period of forty-one years. The first boat that Mr Tucker used was the old ferry boat that plied across the river before the erection of Grindleton Bridge. That boat was carried down river on a "flood tide" navigated by two venturesome youths, who got into dire straits on their perilous journey and were finally upset at a point in the river known as "Dangerous Corner". With the help of some quarrymen the craft was floated again and Mr Tucker acting as pilot steered her safely into harbour. Time rolled on, and Mr Tucker realised that there was the making of a pleasant resort in this portion of the valley, so he determined to suit thought to action. In 1882, the first tea room was erected, and many boats were added to the ever increasing small fleet until the number now is far in excess of what was at one time ever dreamt of. The charms of the place still entice enthusiastic support from all parts of the valley, and Brungerley Bridge is a self advertising medium today.

Before 1801 the hipping stones so fateful in the life of King Henry VI were the only route across the river, while horses and carts used the ford. Then in 1801 woodwardens were appointed "to ascertain what wood would be needed to make framework for setting the hipping stones in at Brungerley and to get it from town woods." A bridge became vital at this time as industry was developing downstream towards Edisford, and the water backed up against a dam, thus raising the level at Brungerley and covering the hipping stones, especially after rain. The first flimsy structure did not last long, being destroyed by floods and replaced in 1816 by the present bridge. During the 1939–45 war several bridges sprang up overnight as the Royal Engineers trained their bridge builders

Brungerley Bridge in 1905, with pleasure boats on the river and pleasure-seekers on the bank.

hereabouts, and some of their poured concrete still remains. My last visit was on a gentle autumn morning when I walked from West Bradford alongside the disused quarries, when the riverside alders seemed full of feeding birds, including long tailed tits and siskins, while the first fieldfares and redwings of the back end of the year gorged themselves on hawthorn berries. Jackdaws called from the old quarries which in summer are such a delight to orchid lovers.

Just downstream of Brungerley is Waddow Hall, now put to good use by the Girl Guides, but which is better known because of a much more dangerous female. By the river in front of the hall is Peg O' Nell's Well and a headless statue, said to have been decapitated by the mistress of Waddow in fear of the evil spirit. It is thought much more likely that the statue originated from Whalley Abbey. But is this so? Legend has it that Peg was a maiden who fell and died when reluctantly going to the well. She was not well pleased at her fate and every seven years, it was alleged, she claimed the life of someone to keep her company. The legend seems to have pagan overtones. The goddess of water was named Helen, whose memory may have lingered long along the banks of the Ribble. Peg could well be a corruption of Helen (and not Margaret) and the church at nearby Waddington is dedicated to St Helen. She was said to be a British princess born in York, who became a Christian. She was the mother of Constantine the Great, who embraced his mother's religion on behalf of the Roman Empire. The origin of the words Waddow and Waddington comes from Wada, a tough chieftain ruling these parts in A.D. 798. The stained glass windows in Waddington church show Wada in his war paint, St Helen herself and Henry VI in the act of handing the crown of England over to the Yorkists.

The next bridge downstream of Brungerley is at Edisford, but there is an interesting section between the two which local folk know as the Coe, where a weir was constructed to provide water for the now demolished Low Moor Mill. When built in 1782 by John Parker this was known as Edisford Mill; it was five storeys high and driven by a massive twenty-one-foot water wheel, and a short canal was cut from the Ribble to drive it. During the last war the mill was the headquarters of No 1 Training Battalion, Royal Engineers.

The mill was demolished in the 1970s and houses were built on the site. This is a source of regret to all historians since Low Moor was actually a moated mill, so built to keep out those who were opposed to the "new fangled" looms. By 1826 the mill was owned by Messrs Horsfall and Garnett who brought in two cannons which they threatened to use on rioters! Although now falling into disrepair, remains of the old leat and machinery are still visible, as is the salmon ladder which was made at the same time. Locals remember salmon being frozen in to the river at this point during 1940, one monster weighing in at twenty pounds. How about that for a deep freeze? During the winter of 1986 the river was frozen at the Coe, but although I looked I failed to find a free supper.

Edisford Bridge stands near the site of a leper hospital.

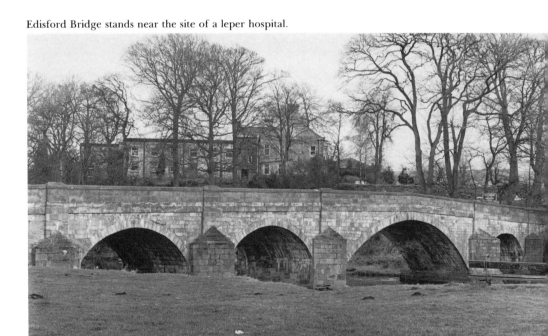

Edisford and Clitheroe

Edisford has always been a vital route between Clitheroe and the west coast and the wooden bridge, probably mounted on stone pillars, was present as early as 1339, and during the reign of Edward III (1327–77) a toll known as "pontage" was exacted at the rate of 4d for a cartload of fish to one farthing for a fresh salmon. Close to where the *Edisford Bridge Hotel* now stands overlooking the river there was once a hospital for sufferers from leprosy—a disease common in the Middle Ages and quite possibly brought back from the crusades. Henry Fishwick did, however, point out that there were pre-Norman leper hospitals at Ripon, Exeter and Colchester. The bridge has been enlarged and repaired several times but it is arguably one of the most important along the length of the Ribble. Before the bridge Edisford was an important crossing point. In 1137 a mighty battle took place at the ford when the Norman forces were defeated by a Scots army and the river ran with blood.

In contrast to the industrialised area north of the bridge, the flat plain to the south has been used for many years as a paddling, picnicking, parking, pottering and playing area and it is still popular today, as the recently constructed car park and caravan site bear witness. Away to the east on a limestone knoll is Clitheroe castle, quite small as castles go, but dominating the little market town nevertheless. Its history and that of the town have been well documented by local historians, especially Langshaw and Weeks. The precise date of the castle's foundation is still not established but can safely be dated around 1086, making the castle one of the earliest stone structures in Lancashire. There seems some justification for the claim that it is the only town in the Ribble valley which was in royal hands during the reign of Edward the Confessor. Langshaw thought that it might have been an ancient British settlement and the name derived from the Celtic words *clyd* and *dwr* meaning the crag by the water, which seems accurate. He also points out, however, that the Welsh word *clyddyr* means a place of defence, and if the Danish word for hill (*how*) is added we have a credible alternative. Yet another possible derivation is from the Old Norse *clitter*, a pile of loose stones, and *haugr* meaning hill. A more bizarre attempt to account for the name is the Old English *clidrenn* meaning a "clatter of noise" and referring to the falling of loose limestone. In 1057 Clitheroe was part of the Kingdom of Mercia owned by Earl Leofric, the husband of Lady Godiva and one of the most powerful nobles at the time when Canute ruled.

Half a mile to the east of the castle runs the Roman road, and it seems logical to suppose that their military mind would have made use of

Evening in Castle Street, Clitheroe.   *Jack Hamner*

the dominating mound. After the Conquest the Norman Roger de Poicton was given Clitheroe, and Orme the Englishman was deposed, but by 1121 the De Lacy family were in control, a position they held for almost two hundred years. Orme's wooden "castle" was then replaced by a stone structure which was thus described by Whitaker:

> Could a curious observer of the present day carry himself nine or ten centuries back and, ranging the summit of Pendle, survey the forked Calder on one side and the bolder margin of Ribble and Hodder on the other, instead of populous towns and villages, the castle, the old tower built house, the elegant modern mansion, the artificial plantation, the park and pleasure ground; or instead of uninterrupted enclosures which have driven sterility almost to the summit of the fells; how great must then have been the contrast, when ranging either at a distance or immediately beneath, his eye must have caught vast tracts of forest ground, stagnating with bog or darkened by native woods, where the wild ox, the roe and stag, and the wolf had scarcely learned the supremacy of man—when, directing his view to the intermediate spaces, to the winding of the valleys, or the expanse of plains beneath, he could only have distinguished a few insulated patches of culture, each encircling a village of wretched cabins, among which could still be remarked one rude mansion of wood, scarcely equal in comfort to a modern cottage, yet then rising proudly eminent above the rest, where the Saxon lord, surrounded by his faithful *cotari* (tenants owing personal service to the lord), enjoyed a rude and solitary independence, owning no superior but his sovereign.

The actual size of the Norman castle was less than an acre, being restricted by the dimensions of the knoll. There was an outer and inner bailey and a keep with a curtain wall and a gatehouse controlling the entrance. The square keep was forty-three feet high and consisted of three storeys, one for storage of food and weapons, the hall for living and the upper floor for sleeping. A battlemented parapet offered grand views in all directions. There would also have been wooden buildings long since gone, as has the "plain" chapel of St Michael. The castle keep was restored during 1985–86, but the layout of the entrance and the keep itself have been substantially altered over the centuries following Parliament's decision to dismantle it. Arthur Langshaw's guide published in 1947 gives a graphic account of events:

> The last turbulent scene in the castle took place after Cromwell had shattered the Royalist army at Preston. The King had been executed and the Commonwealth established. It was now necessary to discharge the standing army that had been created during the war. This was done by disbanding the county militia regiments. There still remained in Lancaster about 4,000 of the Lancashire militia, who had won distinction at Appleby, by capturing a large remnant of the Royalists with many officers. These men were drawn in part from the Hundred of Blackburn and had been led by Colonel-General Assheton and the venerable Colonel Shuttleworth. These men were dissatisfied with the Commonwealth because large arrears of pay were due to them and they wished to see established the Presbyterian form of religion. They refused to disband, and marching through the Trough of Bowland, reached Clitheroe Castle and attempted to fortify themselves there. Major-General Lambert was ordered to proceed there and disband them by force, if there was no other way. Happily for all concerned the mutinous forces submitted and quitted the castle. The troops under Colonel-General Assheton received arrears amounting to £3,400, and those under Colonel Shuttleworth, made up in the main of men of the Hundred of Blackburn, £1,200.
>
> And then the order went forth that made the castle the ruin it is today; it was to be put "in such a condition that it might not be a charge to the Commonwealth to keep it, nor a danger to have it kept against them . . ." Charles II conferred it upon the General Monck, along with other honours, for the part he played in restoring him to the throne of his ancestors. Through three centuries almost the Honour remained in the Lands of his heirs, until by purchase it has become the property of Mr Ralph Assheton, who, appropriately enough, can trace his ancestry down the centuries to the original Lord of the Honour, Roger of Poitou.
>
> But since the year 1920 the castle and its 16½ acres of grounds has become the property of the Borough of Clitheroe, for in that year the rate-payers decided to purchase it . . . for the sum of £9,500, and they opened a subscription list and raised the sum of £15,000 which served to finance the necessary work to make it a public pleasaunce for all time. The area became the memorial garden to those Clitheroe men who fell in the Great War of 1914 to 1918. What had been Stockwell Meadow was drained and turned into a playing field . . .

The old Stocks well, however, still exists and the castle grounds echo to the sound of summer concerts held at the bandstand. The museum in the old buildings with dungeons beneath is splendidly appointed and full of information on Ribblesdale, and the Keep still stands proudly over the main street with its inns — particularly the *Swan* and *Royal* which did a roaring trade during the coaching days. I never visit Clitheroe without thinking that it has a similar atmosphere to spa towns such as Buxton and Harrogate which it once tried to emulate. The remains of the effort can be seen behind Pendle Mill in the spa building, which had a classically designed frontage with gritstone arcades and corbels. The use of these springs, which smell of sulphur, may well long pre-date the advertisement in the *Blackburn Mail* of 1838 which described the spa buildings as neat and offering hot and cold baths, healing waters, dressing rooms and

Great Mitton Hall and the church of All Hallows, one of the finest in northern England.

other convenient apartments. Taking "mineral waters" was a recognised cure for skin complaints including leprosy. I often walk from the hydropathic establishment through the town and down to the river at Edisford. All I need to complete my journey through time is a stick and a leper's bell!

Onwards to Ribchester

The stretch of the Ribble between Clitheroe and Ribchester is scenically interesting because within the space of a few miles it passes through the historic hamlet of Mitton and then absorbs the substantial tributaries of the Hodder and the Calder, both of which are well worth separate chapters in their own right. It then passes through Dinckley and whirls through Salewheel, sweeps along the edge of Salesbury Hall and into Ribchester which has dominated the Ribble since Roman times!

> Hodder, Calder, Ribble and Rain
> All meet together in Mitton's Demain

Before the county boundaries were realigned in 1974 Little Mitton was on the Lancashire side of the Ribble, which formed the boundary with Yorkshire, and Great Mitton stands proudly on a bluff of rock once part of the white rose family. There was a ferry here known as Mitton Boat. Little Mitton has the magnificent hall while Great Mitton has the church. The best way to appreciate both is to begin at the fifteenth century Lower Mitton Hall, now a fine restaurant. The splendid woodwork and original ministrel's gallery have now been restored but they were almost lost during the nineteenth century when the hall was used as a humble farmhouse. It was rescued by Ralph Aspinall, whose family is remembered in the name of the *Aspinall Arms* close by overlooking the river.

On the other side of the bridge we must climb steeply towards the church, look at the building on the right and ask ourselves the question When is a hall not a hall? The Reverend F. G. Ackerley notes "If, as is likely, the house called Great Mitton Hall is on the site of the rectory of 1388 . . . There was no Lord of the Manor present at Mitton (Great) after 1312 . . . The rectors appointed after that date may well have used the manor house as a rectory." It is thought that the present building dates in part to the period between 1374 and 1393 although there have been a number of alterations since.

The nearby church of All Hallows is one of the finest in northern England; the oldest portion is the nave, built around 1270, with the

Mitton Hall in 1905.

chancel being added just before the beginning of the fourteenth century. The impressive tower is mentioned in a document dated 1438, but it is the interior which is such a joy, and the fact that the church has to be kept locked is not a reflection upon the clergy but upon the state of our present rather lawless society. There was a chantry in the original church which was removed to make room for the truly magnificent chapel of the Shireburn family of nearby Stonyhurst, constructed in 1594. It is isolated from the chancel by a priceless Elizabethan screen and within is an alabaster tomb which is a fine example of the intricate carving skills of Roily of Burton and bears the inscription

> Here lieth the bodie of Sr. Ricrd. Sherburne Knight most Forster of Ye Forrest of Bowland steward of ye Manor of Sladeburne Lieutenant of ye Ile of Man and one of her Mats. deputie decutes in ye Countie of Lanc. And Dame Maude his wife daught' of Sr. Ricrd Bold Knight by whome he had issue who died ye 10 of Nov 1588 and Sr. Ricrd. died the 26 of Julie 1594.

We shall return to the Shireburnes in the chapter on the River Hodder, but we must now follow the Ribble beyond its confluence with its tributary and pass on downstream to the footbridge at Dinckley. A stone close by commemorates the opening of the bridge on 10th October,

1951; despite its substantial structure it was severely damaged by storms in 1982, but has been firmly repaired. Dinckley Hall, which dates back to Tudor times, lies snugly at the end of a meandering lane on an important trade route. A ferry service was therefore vital and initially there was a "trows ferry" consisting of two hollowed out logs which were pulled by ropes backwards and forwards across the river. This was later replaced by a rowing boat, which operated until 1951. It was rowed by the local farmer and those wishing to cross had to give him a shout; I am told on good authority that he was stone deaf until a boatload had gathered. Apparently an obligation to operate the ferry was part of the farm lease, and this could at times disrupt more profitable or perhaps essential work on the farm. Apart from the bridge the scene can have changed little since Tudor times; the view from the windows of Dinckley Hall would be familiar to former residents including Dorothy Talbot, the De Cliderows, and also to the old ferryman Thomas Hardiker, known locally as Old Charon.

An easily walked footpath leads from Dinckley over flower-strewn meadows and through Martes Wood—Martes means pine marten, long

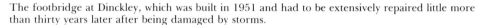

The footbridge at Dinckley, which was built in 1951 and had to be extensively repaired little more than thirty years later after being damaged by storms.

extinct in these parts—to Salewheel. Here the Ribble rushes into a narrow gorge of limestone and on its approach is twisted as it flows and is corkscrewed into a magnificent stretch of white water which is a popular training ground for canoeists desperate to pit their skills against the elements. Birdwatchers and anglers haunt the deeper pools of still water, as do herons, kingfishers and wildfowl. On a bitterly cold morning in February, 1986, I counted 147 goldeneye which had found an area of unfrozen water. In springtime, however, the banks of river and woodland are carpeted with flowers. A steep path leads up to Salesbury, which although attractive and of Saxon origin has no antiquities to prevent us strolling onwards to one of England's most historic villages: Roman Bremetennacum Veteranorum—which we know as Ribchester. Before we continue along the Ribble, however, we must do a little backtracking and investigate the major tributaries. Pendle Hill is an important catchment area for Ribble water and we also need to trace the course of the Hodder and the Calder, which are both important although contrasting rivers in their own right.

The snow-capped Pendle Hill seen from between Barley and Downham.

CHAPTER FOUR

Pendleside

STANDING some 1,831 feet (558 metres) high, Pendle could do with another 169 feet (51 metres) to make it into a mountain, which it well deserves to be as it dominates the towns and villages crouching like faithful dogs at its feet. In the context of this present book it is important, since its westerly slopes are drained into the Ribble itself while those on the east feed the Calder, a major tributary described in the next chapter. When George Fox visited the area in 1652 he "was moved" to climb Pendle and from its flat summit he reported in his journal that "I saw the sea bordering upon Lancashire and the Lord let me see what places he had a great people to be gathered."

Living as I do on the slopes of this whale-shaped hill with its "big end", "little end" and "nick" between the two, I have climbed it in all weathers and in variety of company. One memorable scramble was on Hallowe'en in the pouring rain following revellers up the puddled path to the summit and keeping an eye on the "witches". Locals assault Pendle on witch night, many dressed as Demdike, Chattox or as other members of the coven of old crones. Pendle, used for centuries as a beacon hill to warn of impending danger, was the haunt of the Lancashire witches, whose homes were concentrated mainly on the eastern slopes around Roughlee. In 1612 a group of ugly old women who dabbled in herbs and were not averse to cursing their enemies gained a probably undeserved reputation for witchcraft. Among them, surprisingly, was Alice Nutter, a lady of substance who lived at Roughlee Hall. Many historians think that Alice Nutter was a Roman Catholic who preferred to be accused of attending a witches' coven at Malkin Tower on Good Friday rather than be accused of attending an illegal Mass which would have involved betraying fellow Papists. With her companions Alice was found guilty and hanged at Lancaster in the same year.

An old Dalesman once stopped me while I was leading a group of naturalists around the hill and whispered gently with a glint in his eye "Thee have fun up on yon hill lad but alus remember tha'll larn more in thi' own company than int' middle o' yon crowd." How right he was, and solitary days upon the hillside with only the wildlife for company have brought me so much pleasure over the years, not to mention knowledge.

The sundial on Salem Congregational Church at Martin Top.

I remember snow buntings in January, blackcock in February, mad March hares, lizards basking in the warm April sunshine, dotterels in May, pipits in June, a fine red fox cub in July, succulent bilberries in August, splendid purple heather in September, dippers on the October streams, flocks of lapwings in November and red grouse coping easily in a December blizzard and telling everyone else to "go-back, go-back". Aye, she's a grand old hill, is Pendle!

On the Clitheroe side of the hill we have Rimington, Twiston, Downham, Worston, the Mearleys, Pendleton, Barrow and Wiswell. Although cooler and rather wetter, the villages clustered under the eastern slopes are equally attractive and include Barley, Roughlee, Newchurch and Sabden. Connecting them all is a meandering network of lovely roads dotted with ancient halls, chapels, springs and tiny woods full of spring and summer flowers, while in autumn the hedgerows are ablaze with berries.

Pendle's western villages

The fame of Rimington has been ensured by Francis Duckworth who was born, appropriately enough, on Christmas Day, 1862, and died in 1941. During his life he wrote many hymn tunes, including "Rimington". At nearby Martin Top there is a plain yet attractive Nonconformist chapel. On its outer wall is a sundial that tells us that "Time flies swift away". Middop Hall, although privately owned and difficult of access, is often sought after by urgent and single-minded historians in pursuit of the bits of Salley Abbey which are incorporated into its walls. The same is true of other similar buildings in the Pendle area. Archaeologists also find the area irresistible, and it is along Stopper Lane that we find the spoilheaps of the long-disused mine from which William Pudsay obtained lead, and some of the silver from which he made his illegal shillings. It is surprising to find that lead is not poisonous to all life-forms, and spring or vernal sandwort, *Minuartia verna*, is always associated with spoil heaps.

The walk from Rimington to Downham is remarkable for the sheer variety of both its scenery and its wildlife. The road crosses Ings Beck, which can be followed upstream upwards Twiston or downstream towards its confluence with Swanside Beck, which is spanned by a beautifully proportioned packhorse bridge. Herons hunt for frogs and fish in the deeper pools, dippers breed along the length of both streams and kingfishers are encountered occasionally by the lucky and often by the skilled local naturalists. The most interesting species in the area is without question the Mandarin duck *Aix galericulata*, an Asian species which has escaped from collections and is now breeding successfully in several parts of Britain. Ings Beck itself is also important to historians since it was once the boundary between the ancient kingdoms of Mercia and Northumbria. The old spelling of Twiston reflects this fact, as *Twyssulton* actually means "town on a boundary". Little remains of the old settlement but there are signs of an old mill, and there was once a chapel now only remembered as the name of a farm. At one time the hamlets of Ings End, Lower Gate and Higher Twiston were possibly linked by a string of buildings huddled in the shelter of Twiston Moor. The monks of Whalley had a corn mill at Twiston in 1327. In the seventeenth century a field near Red Syke farm served as a Quaker burial ground.

Ings Beck eases its way around the ancient limestone reefs and past Downham mill, built beneath a particularly fine example of a reef. From the tree-fringed summit the limits of the old mill lodge and leat can clearly be seen. Although the mill is privately owned the footpath passes through the old yard; many of the millstones are still present. This road

71

A limestone reef at Downham, a relic of the time when the whole area was the bed of a warm coral sea.

leads from Downham and swings left past Downham Hall, the home of the Assheton family. Some idea of how long the surrounding area has been settled can be realised by the fact that three Roman roads run close by, and in the wall of Downham Hall close to the gates is a mark indicating the spot where two Roman soldiers were buried. Roman Law forbade burial within the confines of their settlements and so folk were frequently buried alongside roads.

The Hall, which once belonged to a Saxon named Aufrey, was surrounded by a thick fence, probably of hawthorn, and guarded at night. In 1910 when repair work was going on to the church Saxon foundations were exposed, thus proving the presence of a fairly substantial settlement. After the Conquest William of Normandy gave Downham to Ilbert de Lacey. His family held on to it until 1353 when the Duke of Lancaster took control for a short period before passing it on to the Dyneley family, who in 1558 sold it to Roger Assheton. Although the head of the family is now named Lord Clitheroe, Downham remains the home of the Assheton family, a fact commemorated in the name of the public house renamed the *Assheton Arms*, after a period as the *George and*

Dragon. Downham has sadly lost its village school in recent years, but otherwise it has everything which an English village ought to have and has often won awards for its charm. It has a pebble-bedded stream always seeming to overflow with mallards begging from visitors to the adjacent car park. Opposite the village stocks is the church of St Leonard, parts of which date back at least to Norman times. In the fifteenth-century tower hang three bells which once called the monks of Whalley Abbey to prayer. Inside is a font given by John Paslew, the Abbey's last abbot.

A walk from Downham to Worston follows one of the routes followed by the monks, across fields which were hunted by Squire Assheton, who left a diary describing killing both fox and bowson, the old name for a badger. This diary has often been quoted in books on the history of fox hunting because it contains one of the earliest descriptions of a hunt. After passing the lovely old cottages in Downham, many with

Downham Mill, set in a delightful rolling countryside which is deservedly popular with walkers.

73

colourful gardens, a footpath turns off the Worston road and leads past the halls of Little and Great Mearley.

Settlement in the Mearley area seems to have been much more extensive in the past than at the present time. There are some suggestions that it never recovered from a visitation of the plague. There are substantial earthworks near Great Mearley which support the idea of a former settlement. Little Mearley Hall is a fine example of a Tudor building, with one of its windows said to be from Salley Abbey, and over the front door are the arms of the Nowell family and the initials C.N. and E.N. Charles Nowell married Elizabeth, the daughter of T. Walmesley of Great Mearley, in the fifteen-eighties. The Tudor hall at Great Mearley has been demolished, but its gates remain in front of a farmhouse built partly from the stones but by no means as fine a house as Little Mearley. In 1660, the year of the Restoration of the Monarchy, another Charles Nowell of Little Mearley was drowned on the day of his proposed wedding to the daughter of Thomas Lister of Arnoldsbiggin near Gisburn (see Chapter Two). One wonders what would have happened in the history of Ribblesdale if this marriage had taken place and produced children. Perhaps the hamlets of Mearleys, which in 1296 were known as Magna and Parva Merlaya, might have become an important town on the main road to Clitheroe. In Old English Mearley indicates a boundary— perhaps of Pendle Forest.

Downham village nestling beneath the shelter of Pendle Hill.

The footpath leads gently onwards, but before leaving the Mearley area the visitor should look uphill to the "Brast Cloughs" and downhill to Worston. The Brasts were created when water trapped beneath the peat burst forth to create damage to the settlements below and expose areas of dark exposed rock, mainly gritstones. Camden wrote of one such event, "It is chiefly remarkable for the damage it lately did in the country below [about the year 1580] by the discharge of a great mass of water". Was it flood or pestilence which caused the demise of the Mearleys?

Another such burst, which took place on 18th August, 1669, inundated the village of Worston, which lies just below Little Mearley on the Clitheroe side. These days it is a pleasant little hamlet of much more significance than the Mearleys, having a few modern houses and a

A brachiopod fossil, *Pugnax*, from Worsa Hill.

splendid hostelry. From the village one can see a scar—possibly a flood scar—shaped just like a witch on her broomstick; it is particularly obvious at times of snow. The name Worston derives from Worsa's tun; thus the village is Anglo-Saxon in origin, although it is also very close to the old Roman road from Ribchester to York. It is sheltered beneath a massive reef knoll called Worsa Hill, which has long been coveted by the limestone quarrymen but so far has remained intact. The hillside has been seen by the millions who have seen the film *Whistle Down the Wind*, starring Hayley Mills. The hall at Worston, once the manor of the Greenacre family, is now a farmhouse. The last in the line of Greenacres was a girl who married Nicholas Assheton (the one who kept the diary which mentioned foxhunting) in the early years of the seventeenth century. Greenacres is yet another local house with fragments of old Salley Abbey in both the house itself and in the wall surrounding it. In a field behind the main street there was once a bull ring, and the iron hoop to which the baited animal was tethered can still be seen.

If this interesting diversion to Worston is resisted the footpath leads one from Great Mearley to the delightful village of Pendleton, well known to tourists for the stream which splits it in two and for the local pub which is called *The Swan with Two Necks*. A ritual burial site dated around 1500 B.C. has recently been discovered in the area, and the village itself dates back to before Domesday when it was described as a "town at the foot of Pendle". It is probably Pendle's tun, *tun* being Anglo-Saxon for settlement.

The name of the public house seems illogical, but we can understand it if we agree that art and science are separate disciplines and neither can understand the rules of the other! At a time when swans were considered to make excellent eating each of England's rivers had a ceremony of "swan upping" when the swans were gathered up—during their period of moult as they are flightless during this period. Those with the authority of the monarch to dine on the royal bird were allowed to cut notches on the beaks of a given number of swans, any unmarked birds belonging to the sovereign. No swan could be killed by any other person. Eventually a directory of swan marks was drawn up and published in 1482. It is known that the Vintners' Company marked all their birds with two nicks from 1472 onwards. The artist mis-read "two nicks" for "two necks" and here we have the proof!

Pendleton Hall is set back from the village and privately owned. It was the home of a branch of the de Houghtons for nine generations before passing to the Starkie family whose emblem—a stork—can be seen on a nearby building.

A lovely path leads to Wiswell. Down in the valley below can be seen the industrial village of Barrow where the water-filled lodges of the now disused mills are being used by wildfowl and fishermen. At one time the lodges were an important haven for birds including whooper, Bewick and mute swans, tufted ducks, pochard, teal and the occasional rare bird such as a smew. Since the lodges have been taken over by a fishing consortium the birds, and indeed the birdwatchers, are less welcome, even though the area is on a footpath. Close to Wiswell is fine example of a tithe barn, and the stump of a cross stands at Wiswell Shay at a distance of about a mile from Whalley. This was used as a resting place for mourners carrying a corpse for burial at Whalley Church. There is a charter dating Wiswell back to 1193, and at one time it was famous for the quality of its damsons, although little evidence remains today. The real claim to fame of the hamlet is that it was the birthplace of the last abbot of Whalley. A short lane leading from the hamlet brings you to

76

Wiswell Old Hall. Now a farm, this is the birthplace of John, son of Francis Paslew, who was first educated at Whalley Abbey, then sent to university; he eventually returned to become the abbot of Whalley. Although the house has been altered over the centuries, the Paslew coat of arms is still visible, as are the typical Tudor mullioned windows, stone seats, porch and substantial chimneys. A short walk from Wiswell leads down through flower-rich hedgerows and woods and then across a busy road into Whalley, which stands on the river Calder.

Sunshine on Pendle, seen from Downham village.

Pendle's eastern villages—witch country

The best way to see these villages is to retrace our steps to Downham and then follow the road over the big end of Pendle and down into Barley, where Pendle Water forms from a number of tiny hill streams. This trickles down to Roughlee, on towards Blacko and Barrowford, then swings away from Nelson and Burnley before joining the Calder at Padiham. Above Roughlee footpaths lead to Newchurch, Sabden and thence to Whalley; Sabden Brook is another tributary of the Calder.

The name Barley, which means the field where the barley grows, is mentioned in 1323 as a "herbage" of the manor of Whitehough. A clear stream trickles through the village and winds around a picnic site and information centre, ensuring the village's popularity with summer

An old view of Barley, with Pendle Hill in the background.   *J. T. Nutter*

visitors. A footpath leads up into Ogden clough, passing through the pumping works of the North West Water Board. These were converted from one of the two cotton mills which operated in the village. This mill, known as Barley Green, had 200 looms in 1862, but floods severely damaged the building in 1880 from which it never recovered. The footpath continues between conifer plantations and up on to the summit of Pendle with views down on to the reservoirs, which are surprisingly devoid of wildfowl. A second footpath leads through the village to Black Moss reservoirs, which are perhaps more sheltered and therefore favoured by birds such as tufted ducks, pochard, whooper swans, teal, mallard and goldeneye, while herons, dippers, grey wagtails and kingfishers are resident hereabouts.

Follow Pendle Water through Narrowgates, where William Hartley's cotton twisting mill is now converted to a private residence, dominated by a huge chimney built when water power gave way to steam. The old mill workers' cottages have also been tastefully converted. The path continues along the riverside to Whitehough, a hamlet first mentioned in 1324; many of the present buildings, including Whitehough House, are of the Tudor period. Once used as a Youth Hostel, Whitehough House is now back in private hands. Above it is a camp school established by Lancashire County Council in 1938, and children on outdoor pursuits or history trails can frequently be seen filing along the paths. After passing through a couple of fields full of lovely trees and bird song the stream reaches Thorneyholme Farm, once a mill powered by the river, and the old lodge for storing water can still be clearly seen.

This is witch country, for up on the hill above Thorneyholme is Newchurch, while following Pendle Water brings us into Roughlee. Newchurch was once called Goldshaw Booth (Booth meaning a cattle farm) until a New church was built in Pendle in the sixteenth century. It is thought that the tower is much older than the rest of the church, and the so called "eye of God" carved high up on the wall above the door is possibly a relic of pagan times. This unfortunately prevents us from accepting the local tradition that the eye of God could keep a look out while the villagers were at prayer. Under the eye is the grave bearing the name of Nutter, but whether the lady from Roughlee executed for witchcraft actually lies here is open to question. It is reported that the Pendle witches, particularly Mother Demdike, removed hair and teeth from corpses to use in their spell-making and also that a notorious gang of eighteenth century cutthroats and robbers used to bury their loot under the gravestone.

Visitors to Newchurch could be excused for curtailing their visits at sunset, but the village had its "goodies" as well as "baddies". John Nutter did something to establish the good name of the Nutters, later tarnished by Alice. He obtained his degree at Brasenose College, Oxford, around 1578 and became Chaplain to Queen Elizabeth who referred to him as "a golden ass", but for what reason I have been unable to discover. He eventually became Rector of Aughton and Sefton in Merseyside and by 1589 was the Dean of Chester. Jonas Moore, who was born at Newchurch in 1618 and died in 1649, achieved a great deal in his very short life. After a period of tutoring the future James II he taught mathematics at Cambridge, wrote a text book on arithmetic and was instrumental in setting up the school of mathematics at Christ's College, Cambridge. He was also one of the surveyors in charge of the draining of the fens, and as if this was not enough he helped to set up what is now known at the Royal Observatory at Greenwich.

Roughlee, with its boating lake (once a mill lodge and now threatened with closure) and its waterfall overlooked by attractive cottages, has long been popular with visitors. New houses now encircle the old cottages and Roughlee Hall, the home of Alice Nutter. Historians have tried in vain to prove how such a well-to-do woman could become entangled with such a group as the Lancashire witches. It has, however, been noted that Alice Nutter and Roger Nowell of Read Hall (see Chapter Six), the magistrate who committed her for trial, had been engaged in a law suit over some land, and with her death as a witch in 1612 Roger met with no further opposition. There is no direct evidence, but the cynics among us are certainly entitled to raise an eyebrow. If the river is followed beyond Roughlee it picks up a beck draining Blacko Moor at a spot appropriately named the Waters Meeting. On the hill stands Blacko Tower, often said to be the witches' meeting place. In fact Malkin Tower where the witches gathered was sited below the present structure and was almost certainly either demolished or incorporated into a farm building. Blacko Tower on the other hand is a folly built by one Jonathan

Relic of a transport system of long ago, a packhorse bridge still spans Pendle Water.

Stansfield, a grocer who was fascinated by the 1,018 feet (310 metres) of the hill, but in 1890 he decided it was not high enough. He could not see far enough into Ribblesdale and built the tower to get a better view, by adding an extra thirty feet (nine metres).

Downstream of Waters' Meeting is the large village of Barrowford, which although it is busy and looks industrialised is in fact steeped in history, and it is fitting that the Pendle Heritage Centre is sited there. At the junction of the roads to Colne and Gisburn is the old Turnpike toll bar and on the opposite side of the stream is the seventeenth century building with its beautiful mullioned windows now occupied by the

Newchurch in Pendle, seen in an old postcard view. *J. T. Nutter*

Heritage Centre. Two equally fascinating buildings are the Lamb Club and the *White Bear Inn* which both have their origins in the late Tudor, early Stuart period. The Lamb has a typical Lancashire tale to tell. On May Day think of yourself eating a nettle pudding and setting off along Pendle Water and then on from Barley to Twiston Moor in order to celebrate Nick O' Thung's charity. This was an idea put forward by a chap who was christened American Tom after he returned to his native haunts during the later years of Victoria's reign. Starting from the Lamb, up on the hills went the local lads, led by Tom, to eat nettle pudding which was made from eggs, meat, dripping and—of course—nettles. No one was allowed a drink until they had recited the following verse without any hesitation. "Thimble-thung Thistlethwaite who thinking to thrive through thick and thin through throwing three thimbles hither and thither was thwarted and thwacked by thirty-three thousand thick thorns." You would have to be sober to tackle such a sentence!

The *White Bear Inn*, built in 1607, was originally the dwelling of the Hargreaves family. At one time bears were actually baited there. Imagine the house standing in its own grounds with the river flowing through, before the construction of the modern road. On fair days there would be jugglers, dancers, peepshows and snarling dogs snapping at the chained bear—if it happened to be an albino animal then it would have attracted an even larger crowd.

Just before reaching the modern town of Nelson (named after the hotel *The Lord Nelson*) Pendle Water swings away towards Padiham, where it joins the Calder after passing through a series of sewage works. Although modernisation has taken place in recent years there are still lagoons of sludge which attract a host of birds, including the ubiquitous starlings and pied wagtails but also rarities such as the green sandpiper.

Before completing our brief tour of Pendle we should return to Newchurch and follow the narrow lanes to Sabden, where the brook which is named from the village flows down to join the Calder near Whalley. The road leads through Sabden Fold, a hamlet well worth a visit, if only to see the lovely farms and the exquisite Elizabethan Sabden Hall. Sabden itself is an industrialised village; its story is a fascinating blend of fact, fiction, folklore and Lancashire's very own leg-pulling humour. I do not believe that there are many Sabdenites who can actually weave the ginger cake they call parkin, neither do I believe that there are treacle mines which are illuminated by buckets full of daylight poured down the shaft. Richard Cobden, who was partially responsible for the repeal of the Corn Laws in 1846 when he was Member of Parliament for Stockport, is real enough, however; although he achieved national recognition through his politics it was Sabden which gave him his financial security. Politics was Cobden's hobby but printing calico was his source of income, a business which he set up in Sabden in 1831.

A steep road climbs from Sabden up to the Nick o' Pendle, and from here modern hang-gliders leap bravely into space and fall slowly down towards Clitheroe and the valley of the Ribble and the Hodder.

CHAPTER FIVE

The Hodder

DRAINING a clutch of dark, brooding, quarry-bruised hills, several tributaries tumble down to form the Hodder at the Cross of Greet. Looking down on the bridge from the winding fell road, one can see the twisting meander of the river snaking towards Stocks reservoir, fringed by the conifers of Gisburn forest. Behind looms the whale-like hump of Pendle.

The valley as a whole shows how comparatively easy it was to construct the reservoir. To build a dam and allow the Hodder to run in freely at one end, taking in Bottoms Beck which runs through the forest, and then to run out under control at the other, was a perfect solution. No reservoir, however, can ever be made without upsetting someone, especially those who see their homes and places of work, play and pleasure disappear. So it must have been with the residents of the hamlet of Stocks, whose houses now lie beneath nearly 350 acres of water. Only an island marks what was a knoll overlooking their dwellings.

A colony of black headed gulls now breeds here and the winter grass is cropped close by large flocks of wigeon and Canada geese, their dark heads contrasting sharply with the white on the neck. Occasionally they are joined by a barnacle goose, which can be distinguished by its smaller size and by the presence of white on the head. Birdwatchers are drawn to the spot, which is now open as a nature reserve, to seek spring rarities such as ospreys and black terns which skim over the water, mergansers and goosanders and red throated divers which swim on it and birds of prey which haunt the huge fringing belt of conifers. The area has recently been opened for angling and its nature reserve deserves its national recognition.

At the side of a road, looking forlorn and deserted, is the old village church, removed stone by stone at the demand of the Stocks villagers who had buried their dead, but did not want them flooded! The original plans for a reservoir for the Fylde were drawn up before the First World War, but it was 1935 before it was functional. During the period of construction the road network into Bowland had to be substantially improved. By the dam there grew up a shanty town with a population of many hundreds, reminiscent of that at Batty Green at Ribblehead.

From the dam the Hodder continues its interrupted journey towards

Slaidburn. Oyster catchers and common sandpipers breed near the shingle beds past Hammerton Hall and under the magnificently proportioned packhorse bridge at Holmehead. This was the original home of the Hammerton family which also built Wigglesworth Hall and Hellifield pele tower as a protection against the Scots. There was a dwelling on the site during the thirteenth century, and over the centuries there were gifts to the "leprous brethren" at Easford (Edisford), twenty loads of hay per annum to the monks of Kirkstall Abbey and gifts to their own church at Slaidburn.

Slaidburn to Newton

There is no doubting the antiquity of the village of Slaidburn, which appears in a Domesday survey as Slateborne and probably has Anglian origins. The precise meaning of the word has been the subject of some confusion among local historians; some state that it comes from the Old English and means battle by the stream. My own preference is for a "sheep field by the river". Excavations, particularly by M. C. Higham, have revealed traces of bronze age settlements, while from the Church of St Andrew one can see lynchets in the fields which are cultivation terraces dating back to Anglo-Saxon times.

The church itself is of ancient lineage, although it is such a mixture of styles that it is difficult to date with precision. Parts of the tower are twelfth-century but there has been some repair work in later centuries. During the fourteenth century the west wall began to bulge and was supported by impressive buttresses. At the time of the Scots raids, particularly in 1322, the church was used as a refuge. There are beam holes on either side of the south door, and the huge log which fitted into them to secure the entrance can still be seen. There are similar holes beside the priest's doors, and particularly large ones at the entrance to the tower, which was obviously designed as a second line of defence should the other doors be battered open. Within the church is a three-decker Jacobean pulpit dated 1740, a seventeenth-century chancel screen, and a Norman font which an early nineteenth-century "do-gooder" smoothed off to improve its appearance. The Hammerton chapel dates to 1447 and bears the family coat of arms of three hammers. On the north wall is a carved stone Celtic head, thought to be of a pagan god worshipped in pre-Christian days. There are also a number of interesting stone carvings on the outside of the church along with a sundial, the base of which could well be the old market cross.

While walking round the church on a bright spring morning the sound of children singing drew my attention to the adjacent school which has been beautifully dovetailed on to the old Grammar school. This is in wonderful condition and dates back to 15th May, 1717, when the will of farmer John Brennand of the nearby Pain Hill provided the money for its construction. The narrow road from the church into the village takes us past quaint old cottages to the *Black Bull*, once a public house but now a youth hostel, and across the main street to the *Hark to Bounty* inn. This cosy spot has its own singular combination of fact and folklore. Before 1861 it was known merely as *The Dog Inn* until a local dignitary, out hunting with the hounds and stopping for a meal, heard one of his favourite dogs barking and was heard to say "Hark to Bounty". From the upper rooms justice was meted out by the officials of the district court for the Staincliffe Wapentake, as well as what then served for the county court. Before the inn was built in the seventeenth century justice was done in a building long since demolished, but the site is still remembered in a field called Court House Close. At the rear of the *Hark to Bounty* is a window which is thought to be from the old court house, made up of small diamonds of blue and green glass.

No visitor should leave Slaidburn without looking at its two bridges,

The eighteenth-century grammar school at Slaidburn which still forms part of the village school.

one spanning the Hodder itself and the other its substantial tributary of Croasdale Brook. Until the 1840s one of the village industries was hat making, using the pelts of rabbits which were bred in warrens alongside the Croasdale and were pegged out to dry on the village green. Curing was done using lead salts. There were many mines around the village, as indicated in the yet unpublished writings of B. H. Lee. While rubbing lead salts into pelts some workers probably absorbed lead into the blood stream, damaging their brain cells; the phrase "mad as a hatter" may well be tragically accurate! The car park by the bridge over the Hodder is a fine spot to begin walks into the lovely rolling countryside of Bowland.

Two delightful roads lead from Slaidburn to Newton, the longest and most picturesque being alongside Croasdale Beck via Laythams, cutting across the line of the old Roman road before dropping gently into Newton at a point near the Friends' Meeting House, which dates to 1767. On the opposite side of the road is the Quakers' burial ground, sited on a breezy bluff and fringed by a shelter belt of fine trees. For a sect which had to put up with so much persecution it is comforting to think that its members are resting in such a peaceful setting. John Bright was a Quaker educated at Brabin's school in Newton—his initials are carved in the

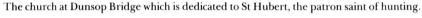

The church at Dunsop Bridge which is dedicated to St Hubert, the patron saint of hunting.

Meeting House—who achieved fame by being instrumental, along with Richard Cobden from Sabden, in the repeal of the Corn Laws in 1846.

Newton was known to the Romans and set on an ancient road from Lancaster to Ribchester. There was a ford across the river near the site of the present bridge. The stone, which looks quite pink in places, is freestone brought from Kitcham and Birkett. A riverside stroll signed from the bridge leads to Foulscales. From the name it sounds as if this could have had a sulphur spring, but the farm of the same name has a very peculiar extension on its south side which might indicate another kind of pollutant. There was thought to have been a fourteenth-century monks' hospice here, and the extension may be their reredorter, which is a "long drop toilet". The doorway of the hospice is incorporated in the nearby farm of Longstripes. Footpaths from the bridge also lead to Easington, where the remains of Roman paving has been discovered, and through a belt of trees to Dunmow Hall, close to which in the late nineteenth century the Hodder was canalised to provide work for the unemployed.

Dunsop Bridge

An old Dalesman, Mr W. J. Martin, recording his youth, wrote of his experiences of Dunsop Bridge in the 1880s, noting that:

> At that time Mr Eastwood was at Thorneyholme. A good many prize cattle were kept there, of the noted "Butterfly" breed. Mr Hazelwood (or Hazeltine) was at the Root stud; Mr Tom Stead was the blacksmith; and a Mr Gornall was, I believe, some sort of factor or steward. And now for the walk up the valley. Entering the gate by the Post Office and following the bank of the steam through the three fields I came to Holme Head, where in my time, I saw the noted racehorse "Kettledrum"; I think the groom was a Mr Woods. The place is very much altered, as now it consists of several cottages, tenanted by employees of public authorities. Next is Bishop's House—why Bishop's I could not clearly learn; maybe I did not come across the right people.

Perhaps we can throw some light on this subject by following the road towards the Trough of Bowland until we reach St Hubert's church, a short distance from the village. I doubt if there is another church in the land which was financed from the winning of a horse race. St Hubert was the patron saint of hunting, and a horse named Kettledrum was trained in the area and won the coveted Derby in 1861 at the long odds of 16–1. Many a local lad took money from the bookmakers on race day. The church was consecrated in 1865 and the graveyard is dominated by a sculpture of a white angel as a memorial to the Catholic Towneleys of Burnley who owned the horse. The roof carried a weather vane in the form of a horse, and there were even pictures of Kettledrum on the ceiling. What a bargain old Kettledrum was! Charles Towneley and his friend from Leighton Hall, Mr Gillow (of the furniture family), bought him from Ireland for £5.

But what of the Roman Catholic Bishop referred to by Mr Martin? Near the gate is a fine carved gravestone which bears the inscription:

> Pray for the soul of Richard Butler Roskell, Doctor of Divinity. He was born 11 August 1817, consecrated bishop of Nottingham 21 September 1853. Translated to bishoprick of Abdera 5th July, 1875. Died 27 January 1883. Jesus Mercy. Mary Help.

Richard was the youngest son by the second wife (Anne) of Robert Roskell of Gatacre. The family moved first to Garstang and then to

The tomb of Bishop Richard Butler Roskell in the churchyard at Dunsop Bridge.

Liverpool, where a living was earned from making watches. Richard was educated first at Ushaw College (1825) and then in 1832 entered the English College in Rome. He was ordained in 1840 and was appointed to St Augustine's, Manchester, in 1842. In 1851 he was Vicar General to Dr Turner, who was appointed the first Bishop of Salford. By 1853 Richard was considered worthy of his own bishopric and was consecrated at Nottingham by Cardinal Wiseman in 1853. Overtaken by ill-health, he resigned on a pension termed *Abdera in Partibus* and after a couple of years in Wales returned to Bowland and died in 1883. It is perhaps a reflection of the times that it was easier to discover the history of Kettledrum than that of Bishop Roskell!

The walk along the line of the Hodder from Dunsop Bridge to Whitewell is unspoilt. The stream is now large because it receives the waters of the River Dunsop dropping from the Trough of Bowland and Langden Beck, on which is sited a trout farm. This does not concentrate upon fish for the table but on the production of trout and salmon to stock rivers. A field path leads from Dunsop Bridge to Burholme Bridge via a farm of the same name. This is a lovely path in the summer with the purple of self-heal contrasting with the speckled white of the daisies and the different blues of forget-me-not, brooklime and germander speed-well. As the farm is passed a number of conspicuous bumps and ridges mark the site of a sizable hamlet, and all that remains of what was once a forest chapel is a stone that may have been an altar and a carved corbel.

Whitewell and Chipping

A few cottages, an impressive inn beloved of fisherman and the forest chapel of St Michael mean that Whitewell is a small compact spot, but what is lacking in size is more than compensated for by the beauty of its setting. Built on a platform overlooking the sweep of the river and richly clothed in trees, Whitewell is truly a hamlet in the forest. The church probably originated as a chapel of ease, but the present building was constructed in 1817. There was certainly a chapel here before 1422. Parts of the inn look Tudor, despite bearing the inscription 1836, and like Slaidburn, Whitewell was the location for the Forest courts. Poachers

Trees give the village of Whitewell a setting which more than makes up for the limitations of size.

are still discussed by anglers based at the hotel. Deer (red, sika and roe) still occur in the forest, which is seen at its best on the narrow winding road to Doeford Bridge, with its own evocative reference to these beasts. Here the Hodder is joined by the River Loud which rises on the hills above Chipping, one of northern England's most delightful and unspoiled villages.

Chipping lies in the valley of the River Loud, but has its own babbling brook and is protected in a fold between the Bleasdale and Longridge fells. Although the spelling of Chipping has shown variations over the centuries there is no doubt that the word means market, and this was mentioned in Domesday Book in 1086. In the old days Chipping was surrounded by marshland not at all suitable for building, yet the rocky knoll on which the church now stands was ideally sited for both market and church. The market cross would also have been here. Just inside the churchyard gate, reached by flight of stone steps, is a sundial dated 1708 and bearing the initials of the churchwarden at the time. The step on which the sundial stands is thought to be the base of the old cross.

The local children know the steps of the church and the iron gates to which they lead very well because it is here that they carry out their "perrying". As a wedding in the church draws to its close the gates are tied with string and the couple are not allowed to pass through until they throw money down the steps. When the youngsters have scrambled for this they untie the string and the gates creak open.

Although Domesday Book does not mention a church at Chipping, a document entitled *Status de Blagborneshire* states "In 597 Whalley Parish was comprised of all Blagborneshire and all Bolland and so it was for many years. The number of believers increasing in those parts, churches were built at Chepen, Blackburn and Ribchester, the parishes of these churches being clearly marked out." Chipping seems to have been separated from the parish of Whalley in 1041 during the reign of Edward the Confessor, and the present stone church was in existence by 1240. Before this the building would have been of wood or even wattle and mud, with a thatched roof. The present tower dates to about 1450 and appears to have been disturbed little, if at all, during major internal restorations which were carried out in 1506 and again in 1873. Before this last restoration the church had a sunken chancel, a most unusual feature that can also be seen at Ribchester. In the north wall of the Sanctuary can be seen a recess which was at one time an ancient doorway.

St Bartholomew's Church at Chipping and the gates which are tied up every time there is a wedding.

90

Opposite this on the south wall is a twelfth-century piscina, used by the priest to wash the sacred vessels after Holy Mass. The drain at the base can no longer be found, but a further connection with pre-Reformation days can be seen in the Holy Water stoups used by the congregation to bless themselves, which are spread liberally around the church. The remains of two chantries also survive, although they were efficiently removed at the Reformation. Chantries were used to say Masses for the souls of influential families, but they played no part in services of the Anglican church.

There is a complete list of the Rectors of Chipping, but we do not know much more than their names. It is clear that some did not even set foot in the building but were quite happy to leave the day-to-day running of the church to curates, while they collected the rich income afforded by the living. Thomas Clarkson held Chipping from 1721 to 1738 but he was also Rector of Heysham, where he is buried. He did, however, do some good by installing a three decker pulpit, which was replaced by the splendid pulpit fashioned from Longridge Stone that now graces the church. John Milner, the incumbent from 1739 until 1777, was a friend of John Wesley, the founder of Methodism. In 1751 Milner and Wesley journeyed from Bolton to Ribchester and from there to Chipping. The two must have been very fit, for the next day they rode off to Ambleside. Milner was still with Wesley in 1752 when he preached in Ulverston and on 6th June of that year Wesley noted in his diary that he preached at Chipping church and "The people were all attention". Eventually Milner was called before his bishop to explain his journeyings, but his account appears to have been accepted. He was buried in the chancel of his church in 1777.

Two prized possessions are an ancient chest and an Elizabethan silver chalice. The seventeenth-century chest came from St Bartholomew's Hospital in London and was given to the church by a parishioner in 1973. The only connection appears to be that both buildings are dedicated to the saint. Beside the chest stands an ancient stone, believed to be Saxon. Although its function is not clear the presence of a drain hole leads me to believe that it is a font. The Elizabethan silver chalice was presented to the church in 1604. The present vicar, the Reverend Fred Cheall, tells me that he has never seen it, and neither have any of his parishioners; as it is so valuable it is kept locked up in a bank vault. Less attractive but equally fascinating and more permanent features of the church are five medieval carvings of heads on the second pillar of the north arcade showing a donkey, a woman with a hare lip, a man with a cleft chin, one with a long tongue poking out and a fifth who is quite handsome. Some think that they may have been designed to frighten away the devil. I wonder, however, if some mason with a wicked sense of humour was depicting himself and his "friends".

St Bartholomew's has a splendid example of modern stained glass in the east window, dedicated in 1966 to the memory of John Berry, chairmaker. It depicts all the tools of the chairmaking trade, and the sources of power—namely water and fire. It also shows chairs of Lancashire spindle-back design, examples of which can be seen in the church itself.

A short walk from the church down a lane with steep hedges, ideal cover for birds whatever the season, leads to Berry's furniture factory. The sound of the sawmill and the smell of timber and sawdust fill the air. Huge trunks of beech and ash are fed into one end of the factory, once a cotton mill, and finished furniture, mainly chairs, emerges from the other end, to be packed into one of many vans delivering to all parts of the country. Orders are taken from many parts of the world, especially the United States.

Cottage-based industries were a feature of the village. Individual craftsmen had been producing chairs for more than 200 years when in

John Brabin's school at Chipping where the village youngsters now gather to drink coffee and play pool and snooker.

1840 John Berry organised a factory. The forest of Bowland had ample timber for its initial needs and Chipping Brook, tumbling down from Parlick Pike, provided the power to turn a mighty water wheel. The old wheel has long since been made redundant as a source of power, but it is still intact within the body of the busy factory.

At one time Chipping Brook provided power for five mills. One now serves as a cheese factory, another is used as the chair factory and a third has been splendidly preserved as part of the Water Wheel Restaurant. The restoration was carried out by Charlie Smithies, who for many years kept the post office, in the most historic house in Chipping. Here lived John Brabin, who worked hard as a wool merchant, died a bachelor and left money to set up and maintain a school. His will makes fascinating reading as it not only shows the man's generosity but gives a valuable insight into the social conditions of the time:

> In the name of God Amen, ninth day of April in the year of our Lord 1683, I John Brabin of Chipping in the County of Lancaster, Gentleman, being infirm of body, but of good and perfect rememberance, praised be God for the same, do make and ordain my last will and testament . . . After my funeral expenses shall be discharged I give unto my dear brother William Brabin, if he shall be still living after my decease . . . fifty pounds to be sent to him in gold if it can be procured. If my brother not be living then it is my will and mind that my executors shall dispose of the said fifty pounds for the putting forth of such poor children to trades or calling as they shall think fit within Chipping, Thornely and Bleasdale . . . To Grace Kirk my late servant forty shillings, to her sister Elizabeth Hodgkinson of Preston the same and to Richard Boulton the sum of £10 to be set aside for him until he reaches the age of twenty-one . . . To Mr Richard Whyto minister of Chipping my best shoes, my best slippers, my book called "The Works of Josephus" and ten pounds in money . . . To Grace Kirk my old shoes and slippers . . . To Thomas Whaley son of Benjamin my book of Halls Contemplations and Ten pounds . . . To Christopher Parkinson my desk, my hat and hat case, two brushes, my best bands and a handkerchief and to his wife my best candlesticks and snuffers . . . The remainder of my personal estate shall be used to build a schoolhouse in a convenient place in the Parish of Chipping, and an almshouse to house the schoolmaster and scholars and also some of the poor people of the Township of Chipping. It is my will and mind that if any schoolmaster is not careful in teaching the said children then another shall speedily be appointed . . . The tenement . . . shall be maintained and books and clothes for the use of poor children shall be obtained.

Some value of seventeenth century money can be realised when we see that Brabin left a total of £725 12s. 3d. His will mentioned far too many of his family and friends to have included them all in the extract quoted above.

Brabin's school still stands on the narrow twisting and appropriately named Windy Street. Although there is now a modern junior school which also bears his name, the original building still echoes to the voices of the young, for here gather the teenagers of the village to brew coffee, listen to records and play pool and snooker. I think the generous old wool merchant would also be pleased to see visitors pouring into his house, now serving as a gift shop, newsagent's and post office. Cyclists focus on Chipping during the weekend and enjoy a cup of tea and a natter at the Cobbled Corner Café, sited between the church and the spacious car park. There was a tale years ago that the superstitious villagers built a wall around a cuckoo to try to ensure that it did not fly away and take summer with it!

The area around Chipping consists of rich green fields with healthy looking sheep and Friesian cows busy converting grass into milk—all this is a far cry from the days when deer were enfenced in the grounds of Leagram Hall. In the Master Forester's accounts, written between 1322 and 1335, details are given of a mammoth operation to dig a ditch eight feet wide, four and a half feet deep with a thick hawthorn hedge planted along its five-mile perimeter. A look at a modern map still shows Pale Park, Buck Banks and Higher and Lower Fence Wood. And then of course we have Doeford where this diversion began.

Onwards to the Ribble

From Doeford the Hodder winds its way through its tree-lined valley, past the ruins of the C.W.S. Dairy, closed in the 1960s and having an uncannily military atmosphere, and then past the modern buildings of Chaigley. A manor house has been present here since 1248, and there is mention in the Towneley Papers of 1522 of the granting of land to a priest. By 1747 the property was in the hands of the Stanley family.

Between the Higher Hodder and Lower Hodder bridges lie some of this lovely river's most magnificent gifts, whether the walker be naturalist, historian or someone of a more literary bent. There is a circular walk which begins at the Higher Bridge and leads through ancient woodlands to the Lower Bridge. Just beyond this bridge the Hodder joins the Ribble. A right turn then follows the road to Hurst Green and Stonyhurst school, before twisting around to Kemple End with its Paulinus cross and back down to Higher Hodder once more.

Hodder woods abound in bird life, but are especially beautiful in spring when wave after wave of bluebells bob in the breeze along with wood anemones, lords and ladies, wood sorrel and toothwort, while on the opposite side of the river are drifts of primroses. Dippers are present but there is always the chance of catching the flashing kingfisher or a patiently fishing heron. The essence of these woods was captured by the poet Gerard Manley Hopkins (1844–99), who was a Jesuit at Stonyhurst,

Stonyhurst School, in its fine setting surrounded by Hodder Woods.

and his introspective nature seems to have flowered along the banks of the Hodder.

Lower Hodder is really not one bridge but two, a modern structure and a hump-backed span built by Richard Sherburne in 1562 and costing £70. The old bridge is just downstream and known locally as Cromwell's Bridge. Once it is seen it is quickly realised that Oliver, who did stay at Stonyhurst in August, 1648, was far too good a general to march his army across it and would doubtless have forded the Hodder at this point. Below Cromwell's Bridge lies the modern building of Winckley Hall, once serving as a nursing home but now privately owned. It is here the Hodder merges into the Ribble and loses its identity. At one time the house belonged to the Knights Hospitallers, whom we shall meet again at Ribchester, but by the early fourteenth century the de Winckleys were in residence and it eventually became absorbed into the lands of the mighty but ill-fated Sherburne family.

At this point we have come to the end of our journey down the Hodder, but it would be wrong to leave out an account—however brief—of Stonyhurst, one of the finest buildings in the whole of England. This is best reached by continuing the circular walk back to the Higher Hodder bridge. As you tread the road, and perhaps smell the tar if the day is hot, think about John L. McAdam, who in 1826 first tried out his construction methods on this very stretch. At Hurst Green, which although a quiet village today once throbbed with industry, particularly bobbin mills, turn right and pause in front of the Sherburne Almshouses. Read the inscription which tells us that they were built in 1706 at Kemple End, which is three and a half miles away near Higher Hodder. Confused? What happened is that in 1946 the building was dismantled, each stone being numbered, and reassembled on the present site, the so-called Sherburne cottages making a cosy home for the estate workers. Continue past the almshouses along a narrow road, and a right turn brings Stonyhurst mansion into view at the end of a long causeway, looking very much like a French palace. Stonyhurst has had an exciting and fruitful history after a very unfortunate beginning. Let William Dobson's Victorian eloquence set the scene for us.

> In the valley of the Ribble there are many old halls, once the abode of knightly families, who kept up the rude hospitality of the middle ages among their retainers and dependants, but which are now the homesteads of industrious farmers. How few there are of these mansions which yet remain even in the possession of the descendants of their ancient lords! There is one hall overlooking the valley of the Ribble which, like so many others, has passed from the family of its ancient possessors but which has not been degraded, as many consider it, by becoming the home of a tiller of the soil, but has been converted into the headquarters of a powerful religious community, and has become one of the most influential educational establishments in the country. I allude to Stonyhurst, the residence of the Sherburnes in days of yore and now the college of the fathers of the Society of Jesus. And a stately pile it is; and what a commanding site it occupies! Rising on the slope of one of the spurs of Longridge Fell, its eminence renders it a conspicuous object along a vast extent of country, and the views it commands are among the most lovely in the valleys of the Ribble, the Hodder and the Calder.

The first documentary evidence of the family concerns Robert de Shyrreburn who held the manor of Hameldon near Burnley, close to the Calder, and he died in 1261. His grandson achieved higher rank; he was Sir Robert de Sherburne. Sir John de Sherburne was with Edward III at the siege and capture of Calais in 1347 but his son Sir Richard produced no male heir. One of his daughters married Richard de Bayley around 1378; Richard adopted his wife's name and added his own coat of arms to hers. It would seem that Stonyhurst was owned by Richard de Bayley who obtained a licence to build an oratory there in 1372. This is supported by Whitaker who was of the opinion that the de Bayleys obtained the land from one Henry de Wath. A series of arranged marriages strengthened the influence of the Sherburnes, and by the time of Henry VIII they were a great power in the district. The family were staunch Catholics but proved resilient in the face of political changes, and it was the failure of the male line which brought the Sherburnes to an end. The infant son of Sir Nicholas Sherburne died in 1702 apparently from eating yew berries, and the grief-stricken family lost interest in their mansion which was being re-built at that time. When Nicholas himself died in 1717 the property passed to his daughter, who had married the Duke of Norfolk, and then after her death to the Weld family. In 1794 Thomas Weld leased Stonyhurst to the Jesuits and once Thomas Weld, junior, had himself become a priest, and later a cardinal, the future of the school was assured.

Distinguished old boys include Sir Arthur Conan Doyle; it is said that many of the scenes from *The Hound of the Baskervilles*, published in 1902, were written with local moorlands in mind. The actor Charles Laughton, who immortalised Captain Bligh of the *Bounty*, and Charles Waterton the naturalist were also grateful to the Jesuit support and training, but a more permanent reminder of the school's traditions is found in its possessions. These include Sir Thomas More's cap with a silver seal, Henry VIII's cloak which he wore for his meeting with Francis I of France on what has become known as the Field of the Cloth of Gold, and a jewelled prayer book which Mary Queen of Scots carried with her to the scaffold. There is no doubt that the family made good use of the priest hole over the front entrance and concealed by the armorial bearings, for Catholics were not popular from the time of Elizabeth I. It is a wonder that Mary's prayer book, which contains a lock of her hair, survived intact and was not burned or torn up. Bibliophiles will delight at the sight of the original copy of the Lindisfarne Gospel.

Schools should always be judged upon academic achievements; during the nineteenth century a reputation for scientific studies both natural and physical was established. Meteorological observations were of such a high standard that in 1867 Stonyhurst was chosen as one of seven observatories by the Board of Trade. The reputation was so high by the 1870s that Fathers Perry and Sidgreaves were world authorities on heavenly bodies, and were officially in charge of observations of eclipses and events such as the transit of Venus. Father Rowlands was also a fine physical scientist during the middle of the present century. By the 1970s, however, the observatory was in disrepair; it was restored with the co-operation of the East Lancashire Astronomical Society, largely through the driving force of Philip Horrocks.

I once overheard a visitor to Stonyhurst whisper to her friend "What a place to teach in!" I would prefer to say "What a place to learn in". This applies particularly to a student of the River Ribble who is so close to the mother river and two of her major tributaries, the lovely Hodder and that much-maligned river the Calder.

CHAPTER SIX

The Lancashire Calder

MANY years ago the towering moors above Burnley between Holme-in-Cliviger and Portsmouth on the outskirts of Todmorden were eagle country. Here it is that the infant Calder eases clear and cool from a moss-fringed spring. The eagles have long gone and the river has not travelled far before it becomes stained by human activities. The sweet trout which were caught so close to the kitchens of the Whitakers of Holme, the Towneleys of Towneley, the Shuttleworths of Gawthorpe and the Nowells of Read disappeared entirely during the industrial revolution when local coal powered the cotton mills, bleach and dye works and a host of minor industries polluted the streams around Burnley. Things are slowly improving and neither the historian nor the naturalist should shirk from the eighteen-mile journey from source to Calder's meeting with the Ribble.

The dialect writer Edwin Waugh described the scene before him in the year 1844:

> At present the road on both sides is well covered with vegetation; larch, mountain ash, and birch trees appear at every step—the result for the most part, of a laudable effort on the part of Dr Whitaker who in the interval between the years 1784 and 1799 planted 422,000 trees on his estate of Holme, cutting at the same time pathways along the plantations several miles in circuit, which exhibit many interesting views. As the district abounds in coal, the works which are built, and the employments which proceed for procuring that mineral, have in measure driven away the crowds of hawks which from time immemorial inhabited there as secure retreat; and even the pair of noble rock eagles mentioned by Whitaker as having "far longer than the memory of man runneth" defied what time, age and yet more destructive sportsmen could do against them, have all disappeared before the unsparing spirit of trade.

A look at the map will soon show that Eagle Crags were a feature of the hills. It will also show how secluded the manor house at Holme must have been before the modern road was constructed and traffic increased. The area began as a grange for the Abbey of Kirkstall but the word Cliviger derives from the Saxon *clivercher* or *clivacher*, which means sloping acre, and this description is as true today as it was all those centuries ago.

The Whitaker family was beginning to make its presence felt in Holme-in-Cliviger when Richard de Whitaker arrived from High

Whiteacre near Padiham in 1340. A series of arranged marriages followed, first into the Towneley family and then into the Nowell family of Read. Alexander Nowell, a powerful religious figure during the reign of Elizabeth, soon recognised the genius of his young nephew William Whitaker. The lad was educated first at St Paul's School and then at Cambridge, where he became a professor, but years of study took their toll and he died on his way back to Holme on 5th December, 1595. It is likely that he might recognise parts of the present building which is timbered Tudor, but in 1603 two stone wings were added and substantial alterations were carried out in 1717. The real character of the house, as suggested by Edwin Waugh, was created by the Rev Dr Whitaker, the chronicler of the history of Whalley, Craven and Richmondshire. With meticulous care he planned the tree-lined walks around his estate, beavered away at historical documents and ministered to the Church of St John at Cliviger. I have often thought of him bent over his desk and writing by candle light until the pink flush of dawn coloured the Calder valley. Not so! The good doctor employed a number of secretaries to summarise diaries and documents and by all accounts did not always return these to their rightful owners. He has been accused, probably with justification, of losing the original diaries of Nicholas Assheton, the fox-hunting squire of Downham.

During his working life at Holme, Whitaker was also vicar of St John's Church, built in 1788 on the site of a chantry. Whitaker took over here in 1796. The church, situated opposite the *Lamb Inn*, is a useful starting point for a walk up on to the Long Causeway, running along the ancient route from Lancashire into Yorkshire. Outside the church are the old stocks and in the graveyard are buried General Scarlett and Lady O'Hagan. Although they sound like a pair from *Gone with the Wind* they both had important roles in the history of the Burnley district. Many people have heard of the charge of the Light Brigade, led by Lord Cardigan, a famous incident of the Crimean War, but there was also in 1854 a charge of the Heavy Brigade led by General Scarlett at the battle of Balaclava. Although his cavalry was heavily outnumbered by the Russians, Scarlett's charge was successful and kept the sea ports open to British shipping. Scarlett was friendly with the Towneleys, whose splendid mansion is only a couple of miles away. The last of the Towneleys to live at the house was Lady O'Hagan, who is buried in this churchyard. Inside the church there are a fine Tudor pulpit and finely carved pew ends which Whitaker thought might have come either from Blackburn Church or Whalley Abbey.

During the late nineteenth century Cliviger thrived—from an industrial point of view—and its mines not only fired its own cotton mills but the coal was of such high quality that it was burned by Queen Victoria herself. As nearby Burnley developed, the role of Cliviger changed from that of a mining town to that of farmland supplying dairy produce, eggs and mutton for the "cotton capital's" rocketing population. It is perhaps ironic that long after Burnley's large mines have closed high-quality coal is still mined privately in Cliviger. Traces of ancient Cliviger can still be seen at Dyneley Fold, which was given by the Abbot of Kirkstall to Matthew de Dyneley. At one time glass was produced here for the Towneley Estates. Mr Simon Towneley, the Lord Lieutenant of Lancashire, resides in a fine house at Dyneley which is said to have been enlarged over the years and was once the gamekeeper's cottage. From here he could look after the game on the extensive, and then quite isolated, Towneley Hall estate.

Towneley Hall and Burnley

The Towneley crest shows a peregrine falcon, which must once have been common in these parts. Peregrine Worsthorne the journalist is a Towneley; he has kept half the family name and added a nearby village to complete his working name. Around the old village green, Worsthorne's modern church of St John is surrounded by a lovely cluster of seventeenth-century cottages and shops.

A footpath leads over fields and past some modern housing to the historic village of Hurstwood lying in the valley of the river Brun, a tributary of the Calder (Burnley was at one time *Brun-lea*). It was on the banks of this stream, legend says—and it may well be true—that the Anglo-Saxons defeated the Danes in the battle of Brunenburh; there is a rock near the River Brun called the Battle Stone. Neither should we dismiss the encounter as an insignificant skirmish. The Anglo-Saxon chronicle noted that:

> The whole day long the west Saxons with mounted companies kept in pursuit of hostile peoples, grievously they cut down the fugitives from behind with their whetted swords . . . Five young kings lay on that field of battle, slain by the swords, and also seven of Olaf's earls and a countless host of seamen and Scots. There the prince of the Norsemen was put to flight.

The Anglo-Saxons had proved worthy of standing up to the warriors from the north, and Brunenburh in A.D. 934 ought to stand alongside 1066 and all that. British history certainly did not begin with William of Normandy! The village has an attractive hall built in 1579 and an ivy-coloured large cottage called Spenser's House. It is here that the poet Edmund Spenser (1552–99) lived for a time before achieving fame and

Tattersall's Tenement at Hurstwood bears the name of the founder of the famous Newmarket horse sales.

fortune—if not happiness—in London and Ireland. Both his "Shepherd's Kalendar" and "Faerie Queen" show more than a trace of North Country dialect. Perhaps Spenser would have been happier if "Rose of Dyneley" had not repulsed his advances! Beyond the poet's cottage is a group of sixteenth-century cottages overlooking a stable yard and called Tattersall's Tenement. These stables were once used by Richard Tattersall, the founder in 1766 of the horse sales which bear his name. Nearby are the *Kettledrum Inn* and the *Fighting Cocks Inn*, both reminders of the Towneley's connection with field sports.

The whole of this area was dominated by this one family, the Towneleys, whose magnificent hall overlooks a meander of the Calder. Geoffrey of Tunley in the thirteenth century built a hunting lodge near the Brun on land given (probably as a dowry) by his father-in-law, Roger de Lacy. Roger's forebears were the hereditary Deans of Whalley. When the abbey came to Whalley the Deans became less influential. In the 1290s the name de Tunley was assumed, and careful management and a series of good marriages increased their lands and influence. In 1415 the Towneleys were prominent at the battle of Agincourt.

John Towneley was born in Agincourt year, married into the Sherburne family, and produced five sons who established seats at Towneley itself and also at Hurstwood, Hapton, Barnside and Dutton. Richard of Towneley was knighted on the battlefield at Hutton field in Scotland, but died soon afterwards leaving a nine-year-old son who soon lost his innocence and grew up to become known as wicked Sir John. Given permission by Henry VII to empark land for hunting around Hapton, he set about removing all who lived within its confines. The Towneleys had always been ardent Catholics and during the Reformation with establishment of the Church of England their motto *Tenez le Vraye* (hold to the truth) was certainly put to the test. The history of the family during the reign of Elizabeth, at the time of the Civil War, and especially during the rebellions of 1715 and 1745 is one of continued support for lost causes, with subsequent loss of influence, income and heads! The family history affected the design features of their home. Detectable still are the features of a Tudor mansion, superimposed on a stout hunting lodge with some splendid Georgian additions, a sign that more peaceful pursuits were occupying the minds of the Towneleys by

Edmund Spenser's house at Hurstwood, where the poet lived for a time before leaving for London.

the time the Hanoverians occupied the throne of England. Look for the lovely Catholic chapel and the number of priest holes. The top floor houses a large barracks where many troops could be housed, while below are the dungeons where the defeated could be locked away out of sight and mind. The vestments of the last Abbot of Whalley are in the museum here, sent for safe keeping at the time of the Dissolution. They are still safe.

After the dust of the 1745 rebellion had settled Charles Towneley made a good marriage to Cecilia Standish, and her considerable fortune allowed him to embellish the hall with fine plasterwork and make a magnificent collection of artwork and marble sculptures, as well as give him the leisure time to become a good scientist. His marble collection was eventually purchased by the British Museum in 1805 for £20,000. By 1828 the religious battles had abated somewhat and the Catholic Emancipation Act allowed the family to take up public office. Peregrine Towneley became the first of the family to be High Sheriff since the Tudor age. A series of early deaths and the lack of a male heir brought the hall into the hands of Alice Mary Towneley who married Lord O'Hagan, Lord Chancellor of Ireland. She found the upkeep of the hall too much and in 1902 sold it on very generous terms to the Borough of

Hurstwood Hall.

Burnley, who have treated it well. Towneley Hall and park are now freely open to the public, and what treats are offered!

The museum offers works of art, including a painting of Kettledrum and a magnificent long gallery; a craft museum has been set up by the stable block, which is converted into a café. A lovely lily pond is overlooked by a magnificent cedar of Lebanon, and paths lead to a nature centre with its network of trails. Bowling greens, a golf course and football fields are all in use. Children can even fish with some hope in the Calder, which is much cleaner these days now the mines have closed and expensive clearing up programmes have been carried out. The River Calder is culverted under the town of Burnley, which was granted its market charter in 1294 and was once famous for cotton and football, both now sadly in decline. Misguided town planning in the 1960s removed most of the ancient inns and market buildings, and the historian must proceed to Padiham to find more of the Calder's treasures.

Padiham and Gawthorpe

The names Padiham and Habergham both suggest that the Calder's fish stocks and wooded banks were attractive to Anglian settlers. The splendidly proportioned Gawthorpe Hall is situated above a particularly attractive bend in the river, and the area has a particular attraction for me since I had the pleasure of having it described to me by the Honourable Rachael Kay Shuttleworth just before her death. An extensive rebuilding took place in 1599 around a fourteenth-century pele tower which guarded the ancient ford over the Calder. Lawrence Shuttleworth watched over the construction of a wonderful Tudor dwelling and delighted the historian because he kept detailed accounts "touching his house". Full details of the stone quarried locally and the timber bought from neighbours at Read, Burnley Wood, Whalley and Mitton are given, and so are details of how long it took to construct the house. Now a study centre organised from Nelson College, the hall houses Rachael's wonderful collection of lace and needlework.

What impressive visitors have sat in the comfort of the Tudor hall under the minstrels' gallery! During the Civil War the local gentry was split—the Towneleys for the King, the Shuttleworths for Parliament.

What, I wonder, would have happened if Charlotte Brontë's husband, the Reverend Arthur Nicholls, had accepted the offer in 1854 of the living of the recently constructed church of Habergham Eaves? The forceful nature of Charlotte's father forbade the move, and a few months later Charlotte was dead. We shall never know.

It is perhaps fitting that Gawthorpe should now be owned by the National Trust and used for educational purposes by Nelson College of Further Education. Dr James Kay married Janet Shuttleworth and added Kay to the ancient name. James, born in Rochdale in 1804, was responsible for setting up the College of St Mark and St John at Battersea, London, which was the first teacher training college, in the 1840s. It was while studying at this college in the early 1960s that I was introduced to Miss Rachael and became fascinated by her lovely home on the banks of a fine stretch of river. Although still somewhat polluted, the Calder is improving rapidly, and one can see why during the industrial revolution it was diverted away from the house. The river soon reaches Padiham which, although it changed during Victorian times when many mills were built, still has fascinating old corners, especially around Gawthorpe Street. Residents are often referred to as thick-necks and water-walkers. The former applies to a lack of iodine in the drinking waters before the days of "iodised" table salt; lack of this element causes the thyroid gland to swell and produce a goitre or "thick neck". The name "water-walkers" is decidedly more comical and relates to the 1840s when it was announced that a Professor Unsinque would walk on the waters of the Calder. A large crowd assembled and saw the boast fulfilled—by a duck!

Old Halls to Whalley

The slow, meandering Calder on its way to Whalley washes close to the grounds of the fine old church at Altham, and the halls of the Starkies at Huntroyde, the Nowells at Read and the architectural gem at Martholme, once the home of the Fyttons and Heskeths. Because of its industrial overtones, with a tangle of power stations and Mullard's television factory at Simonstone, the real beauty of this stretch is seldom appreciated. Cows still chew contentedly at the rich grass of the water meadows and Altham Church is still a haven of tranquillity. The building fits wonderfully well into the landscape, blending with it rather than fighting against it. It is here that the Lords of Altham were baptised and buried. A rather pathetic gravestone tells us that one Nicholas Banastre, Lord of Altham, died leaving no heir. The nave of the church is clearly fifteenth century but much older stones have been found which date back at least to the twelfth century. In the porch is a font "adapted" as a seat which is said to have been presented by Abbot Paslew of Whalley. He also donated a font to Padiham Church, which is still kept in the modern

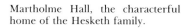

Martholme Hall, the characterful home of the Hesketh family.

building. On a memorable visit to Altham, one of my favourite churches, I sat on a wall overlooking the Calder. A dunnock sang from a low bush, a blackbird from the roof of the church and a wren from a tombstone, while a graceful swallow swept low over the fields in search of insects disturbed from the grass by the feet of the grazing cattle.

Across the river is the fine Huntroyd Hall, still in the hands of the Starkie family, which has held this land since it was initially used as a hunting lodge by the Plantagenet kings. Extensive rebuilding was carried out in 1576 and 1633; it was said that Inigo Jones (1573–1652) played his part in the present design. The Starkies have continued, through civil wars, political upheavals and the inevitable family ups and downs, to keep hold of their inheritance. The neat gardens screened by mature trees, and their farms painted in a traditional red tell us that the Starkies, with their family emblem of a stork, are still very much with us.

Downstream the Calder divides the lands of the old families of Heskeths and Nowells. There are finer halls than that of the Heskeths at Martholme, others with better views and not hemmed in by a Victorian railway viaduct, but none in the whole of the Ribble's catchment area has more character. In a copy of *The Rambler* published in 1905 there is a fine account of the early history of the house:

> To the railway traveller who frequents the loop-line between Blackburn and Padiham, the old manor house at Martholme is a specimen of seclusion and quiet beauty . . . It is a well appointed farm house and the acreage of the farm is pretty extensive and the land is much above the average quality . . . The Fyttons obtained a grant of this manor towards the end of the twelfth century. It afterwards passed into the hands of the Heskeths who had intermarried with the Fyttons . . . the hall must have been built and rebuilt during the successive centuries whilst it was in the hands of the Heskeths and the various costs of arms found in the parts of the fabric seem to clearly point to this . . . The approach is under a picturesque gateway . . . The wide semi-circular archway in the centre of the wall contains a keystone, on which is depicted a shield clearly discernible, displaying the Arms of Fytton accompanied by the initials "R.H." and bears the date 1607 . . . Passing under this gateway, we observe the outer courtyard which leads to a second circular arched gateway in the centre of a two storeyed structure known as the court-house . . . above a sculptured shield are the initials T.H. (Thomas Hesketh) and the date 1561 . . . Passing under this gateway we approach the house itself. There is an oaken door which stood in the centre of the building at one time; for be it known that the whole of the west wing has suffered demolition. In the wall in the front of the house . . . is depicted an eagle with two heads and the date 1577 and again the initials T.H. (Thomas Hesketh). Outside the house there are still traces of a moat and other buildings, which once formed part of a vast pile.

Martholme has had its ups and downs since 1905. After a period as a farmhouse it lay empty and almost ruinous until the present owners began a sensitive and accurate face-lift. Soon the Hesketh home will again be resplendent. It has been suggested that there was once a market here, and Arthur Langshaw mentions one such at Neterton, between Whalley and Padiham, which could have been the spot. There are also the remains of an old corn mill, but these are not obvious. It is interesting that Thomas Hesketh was a keen botanist and recognised as such by none other than Gerard who wrote the famous *Herball* of Elizabethan England.

Read Hall on the opposite side of the river was the home of the Nowell family, who for centuries were reluctantly obliged to pay homage to the Heskeths. A document dated 1429 and written in medieval French, now in the county record office, records this fact. There had been human settlement in this area long before written records began, the south-facing slopes overlooking the Calder having obvious appeal. The name Read may have evolved from *revecht* and *reved*, which means riverhead, probably referring to Sabden Brook, one of the Calder's many small tributaries. Professor Eilert Ekwall, however, in *The Concise Oxford Dictionary of English Placenames* suggests *roe headland*, which may indicate the presence of deer.

There is an ancient road beyond the hall, parallel to but to the south of the modern A671. Some authorities have suggested that this road may have been in use 5,000 years ago, but there is no way of proving this. It is certain, however, that the road was in use in 1800 B.C., and that it continued as far as Bridlington, although not surprisingly the precise route is uncertain. The most favoured theory is that the road followed the Ribble–Aire gap. There was a substantial Saxon settlement which was bound to be attractive to the Normans.

The Nowells are thought to have descended from one Adam Nowell (a useful name for the founder of a great family!) and he almost certainly had a blood-link with one who came over the water with William of Normandy. Adam lived in the thirteenth century and his family followed the usual practice of expanding its influence and property by marriages

A drawing by Carole Pugh of Read Hall before its reconstruction.

of convenience; he himself married the daughter of Stephen de Mearley, obviously another family with strong Norman roots. The marriage not only brought him two fertile sons but also yielded the manor of Great Mearley.

It is from the second son of this family that the Nowells of Read are descended. He had a son named Lawrence who acquired the manor of Read, then owned by Sir Richard Greenacres, thus establishing a family home that was to last until the death of the second Alexander Nowell in 1772. Alexander's debts were so great that the family house had to be sold. James Hilton of Pennington bought the house and associated lands for the sum of £28,000, and in 1799 the property was sold again, this time for £40,000, to the Oakenshaw printing company owned by Taylor, Fort and Hargreaves. Evidently the huge estate was divided up and John Fort had the old manor house completely rebuilt, the construction being planned by a famous Northern architect called Webster, based in Kendal. A contemporary description of the building states that "The prominent feature of the south front is a semi-circular colonnade of six detached columns of the Ionic order, projecting from the building and supporting a railed balcony to the upper storey. The circular form is carried to the roof and is crowned with a low dome." Read Hall during the 1970s was earmarked to become a country club but it is now once more a private residence. This is good, as the countryside around would probably be recognisable to the Nowells of old, even though their original hall has been replaced.

Two Nowells achieved great fame throughout the land. Alexander Nowell was fully deserving of this honour, while Roger had notoriety thrust upon him because of the role he played in the witch trials of 1612. Alexander Nowell was born at Read in 1507 and lived to the ripe old age of ninety-five. This sort of life span is remarkable in any age, but in the unhealthy days of the sixteenth century when fevers raged and plagues devastated it was marvellous indeed. There is also another reason why the death of Alexander in his bed with his boots off must be regarded as one of the wonders of his period. He was a member of the clergy during

Read Hall above the River Calder as it is today.

four turbulent reigns; Henry VIII (1509–47), Edward VI (1547–53), Mary (1553–58) and Elizabeth (1558–1603). With each change of monarch there was a distinct shift in religious attitude, yet Nowell survived and, on the whole, prospered. His portrait hangs in Brasenose College, Oxford, a sure sign of the importance of a man who was Dean of St Paul's and preached a sermon to celebrate the defeat of the Spanish Armada in

Alexander Nowell of Read Hall.

1588. Whenever he was in trouble with a monarch, particularly the fiercely Catholic Bloody Mary, he left the message that he had "gone fishin'," and the Brasenose portrait shows him holding a fishing rod. He is also said to have invented bottled beer; he took a picnic with him on one of his angling trips and placed his ale in the river to cool, and when called away forgot about it. A few days later he returned and removed the cork to find it lovely and frothy.

A walk through the grounds of Read Hall follows the Dean's old haunts and eventually leads to Read Bridge spanning Sabden Brook. Here, on Thursday 20th April, 1643, a significant battle was fought. A large Royalist force including Towneleys, Nowells, Talbots of Dinckley, Shereburns of Stonyhurst and Parkers of Bowland was ambushed by a smaller force of Parliamentarians including Shuttleworths, Starkies, Asshetons of Downham and Bradylls of Portfield. The Royalists were routed; their strength in Lancashire, in the opinion of many historians, was never the same again.

Between Read and Whalley is Portfield, once the site of a Roman fort, perhaps more accurately described as a resting camp. Later the Bradyll family built a hall there. The Romans were not the first to appreciate the strategic value of Portfield. There was an iron age fort here, indicated by the discovery of a collection of bronze objects and two gold ornaments, which are now in the British Museum. Bradyll's Hall was dismantled to build an inn at Whalley but the huge barn remains, a reminder of a once-thriving spot on the hill above Whalley. The winding old road descends past a golf course and Spring Wood nature trails, and then drops steeply into Whalley, one of Britain's most attractive abbey villages.

My favourite approach to Whalley is from Martholme by way of a footpath from Cock Bridge to Whalley Nab. On the opposite bank was the recently demolished Moreton Hall, but in 1829 on the site of a previous mansion. What a pity that this once-splendid building, which had 365 windows and 52 chimneys, had to go. A writer in 1905 reported that a feature of a walk through the grounds "was the sound of bells hung round the neck of the oxen rather after the manner of the Swiss".

I remember well following this route on a sticky evening in the early summer. Flies hung in clouds over the Calder and drifted like whirling mist, overflowing into the branches of fringing trees and into the banks of the river. Their numbers were being reduced by large numbers of birds; I counted over forty swifts snapping merrily away at their supper. They were joined by swallows, house martins and a solitary yellow wagtail. Late June is an excellent time to observe the botanical side of nature, and I recorded a few late bluebells balanced by early blooms of Himalayan balsam, while right on time were earthnut, mouse-eared chickweed, tormentil, the lovely blue germander speedwell and cream-coloured barren strawberry. Birdsong drowned the sound of traffic and bells sounded out from Whalley church.

I cast my mind back to the times of the monks who lived their lives in tranquil Whalley from the thirteenth to the middle of the sixteenth century. The Cistercian Abbey had its origins at Stanlaw in Cheshire in 1178 and removed to Whalley in 1296. Its two beautiful gatehouses remain but the abbey itself was severely damaged because of its resistance to Henry VIII and the part played by Abbot Paslew in the Pilgramage of Grace. After the dissolution the Assheton and Bradyll families purchased the ruin. The Asshetons rebuilt the Abbot's dwelling and used it as their

Read Bridge, delightfully set among the trees.

own home; it remained in the family until 1830. Since 1923 the building has been owned by the Diocese of Blackburn and is used as a conference centre.

Pottery has recently been discovered which dates back to around 300 B.C., indicating an early settlement on the site, but the origin of the name Whalley does not seem clearly understood even among competent historians. Some writers say it means "a field of wells" but Ekwall suggests that *hwaal* means a hill and *leah* a glade or clearing, and I find this latter explanation more acceptable. The Nab derives its name from the Old Norse *nabbi* which means a hill. Coming into the village from the Nab the stroller crosses a bridge over the Calder which was first mentioned in 1317 and which betrays its packhorse origins by the presence of recesses. Look beneath the bridge and you can see that it has been widened on three occasions. Pass the *Swan Inn* which did a roaring trade in the old coaching days when the Manchester to Skipton mail made a scheduled halt here, then retrace your steps a little and pass through a narrow alley to look at the abbey corn mill, not grinding these days but still intact. This alley leads to the Church of St Mary and All Saints, one of the finest in Britain and far older than the abbey.

It was probably Saxon in origin, and in Domesday there is mention of "the church of Saint Mary at Wallei two carucates of land free from all custom". The Saxon church was almost certainly constructed mainly of wood, but the presence of Danish crosses, probably tenth-century, with some pagan and some Christian symbols, is a reminder of the first church. The Normans built a stone church around 1080 but this seems to have been destroyed by fire and replaced by the present building around 1200. Visitors to Whalley church find so much of interest that they keep returning to look at the Nowell family's cage-like pew dating to 1697, or to study an east window designed by Whitaker, showing the armorial trappings of the families of the Calder valley which have taken up so much of this chapter, or to marvel at the real joy of the church, the twenty-two choir stalls. These came from the abbey, and each hinged seat or misericord is beautifully carved. During restoration work in 1866 a slight and amusing mix-up occurred when the abbot's seat was provided with the wrong carving, which causes many a smile. When translated its Latin inscription beneath a juicy-looking cluster of grapes tells us "May they always be joyful who sit in this seat". Another amusing carving depicts a man being chased by a woman with a frying-pan. Perhaps one or two of the monks really did appreciate the sanctuary of their lovely abbey!

Just as there was some friction between Whalley and Salley Abbeys, there also seems to have been some rivalry between the old town and the equally historic Clitheroe. This seems to have come to a head during the late fifteenth and early sixteenth centuries. L. C. Tupling discovered that Whalley held two fairs by custom on the Feasts of the Conception and the Annunciation of the Blessed Virgin until 1591 when a charter was given to Clitheroe. Proclamation was made throughout the country that assemblies at Whalley were illegal, but they were apparently still being observed in 1621 when efforts were made to prevent the fair by the Earl of Derby, backed by two hundred men, which led to a riot.

The only riot these days is the riot of flowers along the Calder's bank as it flows away from the village and under the 2033-foot (619 metres)

Whalley Church.

viaduct, supported by forty-nine arches, which once carried the Blackburn-to-Hellifield railway. One often reads that the Calder feeds into the Ribble at this point and that the river's journey ends at Whalley. What a pity to miss the short stretch of the Calder beyond Whalley, which has a long and fascinating history. It passes through the parish of Billington, over the shallows of Potter's Ford, loops around the fringe of Mitton Wood and joins the Ribble at Hacking Hall.

Billington has its roots way back in Saxon times; the important battle of Billangahoh was fought there in 798 AD. The tumuli found close to the spot are said to be burial mounds but no bones or artefacts have yet come to light. The name of Billington was mentioned in Domesday as was nearby Langho with its ancient church, repaired in 1684 using stones from the ruins of Whalley Abbey. Beyond Billington the river weaves its way gently around the settlement of Chew, once owned by a Saxon named Hugo, the son of one named Leofwine, who was succeeded by the Billington family.

On the next meander is the old river crossing at Potter's ford, which was used by the Romans on the road from Ribchester to Ilkley and York. It is highly likely that the ford was in use by travellers along the green roads long before the legions came to Britain. After passing through Mitton wood with its sheltered banks of primroses and violets and the tiny green flowers of moschatel peeping from a tangle of ash roots, the Calder finally reaches the Ribble at Hacking.

Hacking Hall was the old home of the Hackyng family until absorbed by a Shuttleworth marriage in 1336. In 1258 William of Hackyng gave some land to the monks of Stanlaw Abbey to build a barn, and this amazing structure still stands today. When Anne Shuttleworth married Judge Thomas Walmesley of Dunkenhalgh in 1568 the judge had to fight his wife's family for the estate but finally won. In 1607 he rebuilt the hall.

A look around the local pubs reflects the presence of the families of the Calder. *The Judge Walmesley, Petre, Starkie, Bradyll* and *Towneley Arms*, not to mention the *Stork Inn*, all spring quickly to mind. The ferry was used by priests on their way from Stonyhurst to the church at Old Langho and by locals, many of whom still remember Hacking Boat before it ceased operating in 1954. One boat which was in use until 1938 and which carried fifteen passengers was recently found in a barn at Winkley Hall Farm and is now on display at the admirable Clitheroe Castle Museum.

We began this chapter with a description of the sweet headwaters of the Calder. Industry has robbed it of this sweetness but nothing can dilute the richness of its history or the delight of some of its scenery.

116

CHAPTER SEVEN

The Big Ribble—Ribchester to Preston

TRADITIONALLY the stretch of the river above Ribchester has been called Little Ribble and that below the grand old Roman camp the Big Ribble. Few places on the river have been as well chronicled as Imperial Bremetannacum, but I never tire of reading about it, wandering through it and pondering upon discoveries which may yet be made.

Whenever Ribchester is mentioned the Roman fort called Bremetannacum Veteranorum immediately springs to mind, and it is wrongly assumed that the first settlement dates to this period. It certainly made sense to place a fort at this spot controlling an important river crossing. Evidence is slowly accumulating, however, to suggest the presence of a significant bronze age settlement between three and four thousand years ago; during a dig in 1977 a number of burial urns were found near the car park. The Roman historian Tacitus made reference to the Brigantes and their Queen Cartimandua being present in the area. We cannot be sure of this, but we can be sure that Ribchester and its environs have more secrets awaiting discovery.

Ribchester is the only village situated directly on the banks of the Ribble. The river has changed its course over the centuries, and thus the erosive action periodically exposes pieces of the Roman settlement or artefacts which belonged to the inhabitants. Perhaps the most exciting find was that made by a schoolboy in 1796 who found a beautifully preserved Roman ceremonial helmet which is now in the British Museum, the local museum having to make do with a replica. It is likely that a temporary fort existed at Ribchester before the construction of the main fort in A.D. 79, when the governor, Julius Agricola, was pushing hard into the country of the Brigantes. Bremetannacum Veteranorum guarded the route from Manchester to Carlisle and that from York to the west coast, and was therefore situated at a vital crossroads. There is also some evidence, especially the discovery of an anchor and metal chain ring close to the church, suggesting that the Romans made some use of the river. As many as five hundred cavalry were stationed here and excavations have revealed a parade ground on the site of the present playing fields, and granaries as well as a number of ramparts. Jim Ridge, the curator of the well-appointed Roman museum,

Few archaeologists are as fortunate as Jim Ridge, right, the curator of Ribchester Museum; he has a Roman "dig" in his own back garden.

has located part of the rampart in his back garden—there cannot be many historians who live closer to their study area.

There are many books on Roman Ribchester (see bibliography), tending to give the impression that nothing else happened when the Imperial forces left. The word Veteranorum indicates that retired Roman soldiers were allowed to settle in the area on a pension, and some of their descendants may still be living in the area. The discovery of a Celtic cross and some Saxon pottery shows that folk were living in the area in the fifth and sixth centuries A.D., possibly using the Roman fort as temporary shelters.

A walk through the village beginning at the church and moving out into the surrounding countryside provides a lesson in history from the

Normans to the present time. In Domesday book it is referred to as Ribel Caster, and the Saxons obviously used the river crossing here. The presence of the Saxon cross and the fact that the church is dedicated to St Wilfrid suggests a church of that period. Wilfrid was first Bishop of Ripon, then Archbishop of York, and took a leading role in the Synod of Whitby in A.D. 664, which resulted in the amalgamation of the austere Celtic church into the more elaborate Roman church with the Pope at its head. Ribchester was for many years controlled from Richmond and there was a good road (by the standards of the time at least) between the two through the Aire gap.

The present church dates to about 1100 and has certainly incorporated a lot of stone from the Roman fort. It is thought that the font may be Saxon. During the fourteenth century substantial alterations were made and in the north wall a lovely Norman arch may have been blocked up at this time. A chantry was built serving as a school and a chapel. A wall painting of Christopher, the patron saint of travellers, probably dates to the time when prayers were said at the church before crossing the nearby ford. Indeed the prayers may have been considered vital after a rector called Drogo was drowned while crossing the ford in 1246. The church is rich in fascinating artefacts, and the churchyard also has its

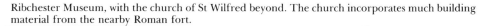

Ribchester Museum, with the church of St Wilfred beyond. The church incorporates much building material from the nearby Roman fort.

share of curiosities. There is a hole in the wall known as a hagioscope, but perhaps better known as a lepers' squint. This enabled the afflicted to watch the service without coming in contact with the healthy worshippers. Just before leaving the churchyard the visitor should spare time to look at the late seventeenth or early eighteenth century sundial, which asks a very pertinent question. "I am a shadow. So art thou. I mark time. Dost thou?"

Our walk through the village takes us along the winding street lined with the cottages of seventeenth-century handloom weavers who before the cotton boom produced high-quality linen made from flax. Look for the extra windows which were needed to provide light. As we move on past the *White Bull* we see a porch supported by four columns which are obviously Roman in origin. The countryside beyond is a naturalist's delight, with flowery hedgerows surrounding gentle strolls between Dutton Hall, New and Old Halls and Stydd.

Dutton Hall, situated on the stark-sounding Gallows Lane, is thought to be near the site of the Anglian settlement of one named Dudda, who has also given his name to Duddel Brook. The beautifully proportioned building with an imposing entrance guarded by ornate gates was built by

The imposing gates of Dutton Hall, built by Richard Towneley during the reign of Charles II.

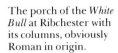

The porch of the *White Bull* at Ribchester with its columns, obviously Roman in origin.

Richard Towneley during the reign of Charles II. This branch of the Towneley family did not fare so well as the Burnley branch and became extinct. The views from the hall, which is now a farmhouse, are unspoiled and the walk down Gallows Lane turning right towards Stydd is gentle and peaceful.

It is always worth while to make a slight diversion and cross Ribchester Bridge into Clayton-le-Dale and have a look at the crumbling ruin misleadingly called New Hall. In his *Rambles by the Ribble* published in 1881 William Dobson has this to say about it. "Not far from the old ford is a superior sort of farmhouse called the New Hall to distinguish it from Salesbury Hall which is often called the Old Hall." The latter, situated on a bend in the modern road to Whalley, was the home of a branch of the Talbot family. If one is allowed to read between the lines of historical documents it seems that when George Talbot married Anne Parkinson of Balderstone in 1665, New Hall was built for the couple. The date, the initials G. T. and a carving of the Talbot greyhound can still be seen over the doorway. Little is known of George but he was one of the governors of Blackburn Grammar School in 1667. A copy of *The Rambler*

Left: New Hall as it was in 1905.

Opposite: New Hall with holes in the roof and broken windows in 1984.

Magazine published in 1905 contains a photograph of New Hall covered in ivy and looking quite habitable. At the time of writing the building is being restored to its former glory.

When we look at the history of the Talbot's Old Hall, which has been constructed partly from the stone of a Roman temple, there is much more excitement, with tales of treachery and skulduggery. In the early years of the Civil War when local families were deciding which side to back, John Talbot called the Parliamentary sympathisers to his house, intending to betray them. Realising what was in his mind, the Parliamentarians turned the tables on Talbot's men and, according to a contemporary account, "pursued them, killed divers of them, took about twenty horses, drove others into the river where the riders were drowned and their horses taken, and having seized upon Sir John's house they found good pillage." The area also saw the end of the skirmish which began at Read Bridge on the Calder, following which the King's men were chased to and harried across the Ribble on April 20th and 21st

1643. Talbot himself was captured in Preston. It has been suggested that when Talbot was released from prison he preferred to build New Hall rather than return to the damaged hall at Salesbury. We shall probably never know the truth of the matter. Salesbury Hall was rebuilt in 1883 and part of the south wing of the old building was incorporated into it.

Before one continues downstream from Ribchester the historic little hamlet of Stydd should always be visited, preferably on foot. Towards the top of a leafy lane are the quaint almshouses built by the Sherburnes of Stonyhurst in 1726 and intended for six Catholic ladies, widows or spinsters, who had to have a reference from their parish priest. Although the Sherburnes have gone the houses are still in use, having been modernised in 1962, and are administered by the Roman Catholic Diocese of Salford. Beyond the houses is Stydd chapel, a mainly twelfth-century structure, whose real gem is a thirteenth-century doorway. Built by the Knights Hospitallers of St John of Jerusalem, the church is probably the only remaining evidence of an extensive medieval infirmary which was doomed when Henry VIII outlawed such staunchly Catholic insititutions. The church is seldom used for services these days and is stark and bare within, but what an atmosphere still oozes from its ancient stones. I am always sorry to leave it, but downstream the Big Ribble still has much to offer.

Downstream to Samlesbury

From Ribchester Church a footpath leads through a farm and across fields of sweet grass to a lovely wood, passing a building known as the boat house, indicating the presence of a former ferry. The view across the river reveals Osbaldeston Hall, which, like so many, now serves as a farm. One should say that this is much better than to fall into ruin. Whitaker in his *History of Whalley*, published in 1872, pointed out that the deer park had been destroyed and that the house itself was but a shell. He also noted that in the kitchen was a bas relief of Hercules, yet another example of the use made of Roman Ribchester as a convenient quarry for building-stone. Since Whitaker's time the house has been restored; perhaps rebuilt would be a more accurate description. The original Osbaldeston family were influential before the Reformation, when they suffered greatly for their staunch Catholicism. Edward Osbaldeston, described as "a missionary", was executed at York in 1594, six years after the failure of the Armada and at a time when the authorities had a fear of another Papist plot. In view of Guy Fawkes' actions in 1605, who can blame them?

Writing about his *Wanderings in Ribblesdale* during the 1940s, William Palmer tells us more about the churches and halls of the area:

> The church at Balderstone was "an ill-endowed chapel-of-ease" to Blackburn. After the Reformation it was recorded in 1559 as "decayed"; about 1646 there was no curate and in 1689 it was abandoned, as the mother church was within easy travelling distance. The Catholics had a meeting place within the chapelry. In 1852 the old church had to be razed and a new structure was built on the same site . . . Here in search of the river, a loose wet track was taken dropping steeply to Sunderland Hall. Up to the lane again, and west with good views over the Ribble deep below. A lane on the right goes down to Balderstone Hall . . . A farmer said that there used to be a ford from the hall to Boot farm but it had never been used in his time.

The first hall at Sunderland was on land owned by the monks of Salley, but after the Dissolution it was purchased by Sir Arthur Darcy. After buying the land of the Osbaldestons rebuilt the hall in 1596, and it was rebuilt again in 1856 incorporating the original datestone. In 1696 the Osbaldestons also rebuilt Oxendale Hall, yet another gem in this area of Ribblesdale, accurately described by Whitaker as a land of small halls and large woods. Only the woods have got smaller, most of the halls now functioning as farms.

As we move downstream into the lands of the Southworths we find that they built two magnificent halls. The first, known as Lower Samlesbury Hall, was the abode of the Cospatricks in the early years of the Norman Conquest, probably around 1180, but the male line appears to have become extinct and the Southworths took over. There is a great deal of evidence that the hall was strongly fortified, but this seems to have proved no obstacle to the rampaging Scots who swept through the area in 1322. The whole village around the hall and church was destroyed. This persuaded the Southworths to build a New Hall further away from the river crossing, less vulnerable to the attentions of hostile forces on the move. According to Ekwall the word Samlesbury derives from the Old English *sceamol*, which probably means a bench or a stool. Samlesbury Lower Hall does indeed stand on a slight ledge above the river. Other researchers have suggested that the Romans called it Minerva Belisima, and as the Angles' word for a fortified place is *bury* we may have the origin of the name Belisamabury which has in later years been reduced to

The unusual almshouses at Stydd, built by the Sherburnes in 1726 and modernised in 1962.

Samlesbury. On the map of the Ribble drawn by the Roman historian Ptolemy, the estuary is called *Belisima estuarium.* A pleasant stroll leads to the beautiful half-timbered New Hall, but before leaving the old village to visit it time must be taken to look around and inside one of Lancashire's most fascinating churches.

On the river just above the church was the old ferry, which was operated by two men as far back as 1379 and continued in use until 1826. There is a boathouse dated 1740; marks have been cut on a window sill, "R. H. 1775" and one about eighteen inches (0.5 metre) lower reading "R. H. 1771", obviously the ferryman's way of indicating flood heights. On 31st January, 1775, the Ribble is said to have suddenly and unaccountably dried up and for a length of three miles people were able to cross "dry shod". Five hours later it ran strong and deep once more, and later in the same year we had the record flood level recorded by "R. H."

For the origins of the church of St. Leonard-the-Less we must go back to the days of Gospatrick, who built a chapel-of-ease around 1185. The "main church" of St Leonard was downstream at Walton-le-Dale and called Low Church. From 1238 to 1537 the church was looked after by the monks from Whalley Abbey but the rot literally set in after the Dissolution. The church was saved only when the third Earl of Derby restored it in 1558. There is still a draw bar, also known as an invasion beam, which could be used to secure the door. Such a beam may have saved the villagers hiding in the tower at the time of the Scots invasion of 1322, although Robert the Bruce did get hold of some plate from the body of the church. The special feature of the church is the box pews, some of which are dated—the oldest 1678—and bear the initials of local people. Some had locks. Out in the churchyard there is even a grave with a lock. Despite this there is a crack in the slab which legend tells us was caused by the angry spirit of Tom Alker's first wife desperately trying to fulfil her promise of haunting him should he ever take a second spouse! The grave is sometimes said to be that of a witch, but if we want to discover the story of the Samlesbury witches we must make the short journey from the church to the Southworths' New Hall, also known as Upper Samlesbury Hall.

This delightful building, once isolated among a tangle of woodlands, was brought close to the eye of the traveller only when the turnpike road from Preston to Blackburn was built in 1826. The hall had then fallen on bad times and Thomas Braddyl of Ulverston removed much of its panelling to decorate his home at Conishead Priory. Samlesbury Hall was then renamed the *Bradyll Arms* and served coach travellers. In recent times Samlesbury Hall has had its dignity restored. Its lowest point was

The church of St Leonard-the-Less at Samlesbury, originally a chapel-of-ease to Walton-le-Dale Church.

reached in 1924 when demolition was proposed, but the Samlesbury Hall Trust was set up in 1925. During the last war troops were billeted in the hall, which did not do it a lot of good. Nature trails run through what is left of the old estate and archers practise at their butts, which must be a real throwback to the old days. The hall is the only one of the halls along the Big Ribble open to the public; it is slowly being restored to its old grandeur and its history can now be shared by everyone. And what a history it is!

Fact, fiction, ghosts and witches, priest holes, fortunes lost and won, all intermingle in the story of the ill-fated Southworths, a family who suffered more than most because of their faith. It must be said, however, that many of their ecclesiastical wounds were self inflicted. Sir John Southworth, after serving Queen Elizabeth as Sheriff of Lancashire in 1562, stuck so firmly to the old religion that he finally died in prison in

127

1595. His dogmatic views even brought tragedy to his daughter who fell in love with a well connected but unfortunately non-Catholic knight. Their story was delightfully told by William Palmer.

> Sir John forbade the marriage, but the lovers had secret interviews among the wooded slopes of the Ribble. An elopement was agreed upon, in the hope that time would bring her father's pardon. The day and place were unfortunately overheard by one of the lady's brothers, who was hiding in a thicket close by, and he determined to prevent what he considered to be his sister's disgrace. On the evening agreed upon both parties met at the hour appointed; as the young knight moved away with his betrothed, her brother rushed from his hiding-place and slew both he and two friends by whom he was accompanied. The bodies were secretly buried within the precincts of the domestic chapel at the Hall, and Lady Dorothy was sent to a convent, where she was kept under strict surveillance. Her mind at last gave way—the name of her murdered lover was ever on her lips, and she died a raving maniac. When three human skeletons were found near the walls of the hall, popular opinion connected them with the tragedy. Ancient folk at Samlesbury used to tell that on certain clear, still evenings, a lady in white can be seen passing along the gallery and the corridors and then from the hall into the grounds; that she then meets a handsome knight who receives her on his bended knees, and then accompanies her along the walks. On arriving at a certain spot, most probably the lover's grave, both the phantoms stand still, and as they seem to utter soft wailings of despair they embrace each other, and then their forms rise slowly from the earth and melt away into the clear blue of the surrounding sky."

Not long after this tragic event the family produced their very own Catholic saint, John Southworth. Born in 1592, John, like many of the family, trained for the priesthood at Douai in Flanders, a college founded by Cardinal Allen who hailed from the Wyre. By 1630 John had returned to preach illegally in his native land, been caught and imprisoned first at Lancaster and then in London's infamous "clink" prison. After escaping and working among the plague-ridden poor of London he was re-arrested, confessed to being a Papist priest, refused to recant and was hanged, drawn and quartered in 1654.

Another Southworth priest—Christopher—turned out to have played a not very Christian role in the Samlesbury witch trial, which took place in 1612 at the same time as the trial of the Pendle group. Seven people from Samlesbury, including Jane Southworth, were accused of bewitching fourteen-year-old Grace Sowerbutts. Under intense questioning the lass eventually broke down and admitted that she had been put up to it by Christopher, who was apparently annoyed that Jane, the young widow of a Southworth and a daughter of Richard Sherburne of Stonyhurst, had been converted to the Protestant religion. There was no way that a family so religiously vulnerable as the Southworths could survive the period of recusancy of the seventeenth century and the Catholic-inspired Stuart rebellions of 1715 and 1745; we should not be surprised that they faded into history, their menfolk hanging from gallows, impaled during battle and rotting in prison. We must leave them here and follow the Ribble downstream, where the tales of treasure and the occult do not diminish but actually intensify.

Onwards to Preston via Walton-Le-Dale

The Cuerdale Hoard, the largest Viking treasure ever to be found in Britain, is thought to have been "lost" or perhaps hidden during a hit and run skirmish with the Saxons. It consisted of gold and silver coins, drinking vessels and jewellery in a wooden chest. Cuerdale Hall, now a farm, was the site of the discovery way back in 1840, and the present occupant is so tired of searchers with metal detectors that he greets them with anything but enthusiasm! What was all the fuss about?

In May, 1840, the treasure was unearthed by two farm workers. The land at that time belonged to the Assheton's. There has been controversy ever since concerning what actually happened to the treasure, as much as where it came from. The *Blackburn Standard* reported on 15th May, 1840, that "The spot where the treasure was found has, since its discovery, been more zealously scratched than any dunghill in the best populated poultry yard." Most of the hoard does seem to have finished up in the British Museum, with smaller representative samples being held in the Merseyside Museum and in the Harris Museum at Preston. Although the amount actually pilfered in the early days following the find might have been exaggerated, there is no doubt that some prominent Lancashire families and a few not so prominent did "keep a memento or two". The lead lined chest contained over 7,000 coins as well as ingots and ornaments of silver, none being minted after A.D. 903 and many bearing Christian symbols. Was this the property of a rich man on his way to or from the Kingdom of Northumbria or was it a Viking war chest? We shall never know, but there is one final and most fascinating tale to tell. There was a tradition in nearby Walton-le-Dale that anyone standing at Walton Church and looking towards Ribchester would be overlooking the greatest treasure in England. This was actually documented in 1810, and those historians who decry legends ought to read the story of the Cuerdale Hoard as a cure for scepticism.

Perhaps we all ought to consider the antics of the Elizabethan Dr Dee with more sympathy. Was he actually up there on the knoll on which stands Walton-le-Dale Church because he wished to locate the Viking treasure, or did he really want to dabble with the devil? John Dee was a man of high intellect and an even higher regard for wealth and power, who claimed descent from Roderick the Great, Prince of Wales. He became astrologer to Queen Elizabeth I, who was more superstitious than is often thought. Dee had an evil reputation for dabbling in the occult, but this did not prevent Elizabeth from appointing him Warden of Manchester College, which later became the Cathedral. This appointment, which came late in Dee's life, was not popular, especially when he became associated with one Edward Kelly, alias Talbot, who may well have fooled the doctor that he was a medium. Edward Kelly had an even

Dr John Dee

worse reputation than Dee; he always wore a cap to conceal the fact that both his ears had been cut off at Lancaster for dabbling in the black arts. Dr Dee and Kelly were so closely tied at one time that they went in for a sort of medieval wife swopping. They were also accused in 1560 of wandering round the churchyard of St Leonard's Church at Walton-le-Dale digging up corpses and performing strange rites. The "recipe" they used is quoted:

> If the ghost or apparition of a departed person is to be exorcised the magician and his assistant must repair to the churchyard or tomb where the deceased was buried exactly at midnight. The grave is first to be opened or an aperture made by which access may be had to the body. The magician, having described a circle and holding a magic wand in his right hand, while his assistant holds a consecrated torch, he turns himself to all four winds and touching the dead body three times with the wand, repeats the following: "By the virtue of the Holy Resurrection and the torments of the damned, I conjure, I exorcise, the spirit of 'person X' deceased to answer my liege demands. Being obedient unto these sacred ceremonies, on pain of everlasting torment and distress. BERALD, BEROALD, BLBIN, GAB, GABOUR, AGABA. Arise. Arise. Arise. I charge and command thee." This being done the ghost will appear and answer all questions.

Without being at all sure of my facts, I'll bet Dr Dee's first question concerned the whereabouts of the "greatest treasure in England". I *am* sure of my facts when I say that the view from the top of the church tower is as fine as any in England and that the historical treasures are equally appealing. Below is the confluence of the River Darwen with the Ribble and also the site of a Mesolithic settlement dating from between 10,000 and 3,000 B.C. There has probably been a continuous human presence ever since. After the Romans came the Saxons, who named it *Waleton*, meaning a "ridge township" or perhaps a settlement of the Celtic British. When the Normans came they added the "le-Dale" to the name and the church is mentioned in Henry de Lacy's charter of 1162. Both this and St Leonard's-the-Less at Samlesbury were administered from Blackburn until 1837, except for the period between 1230 and 1537 when the Cistercians from Whalley Abbey held the purse strings. St Leonard, who died around A.D. 559, was the patron saint of prisoners and the sick. Inside there is no memorial to the sick but there is one referring to a murder! The memorial stone which actually names the murderer is almost certainly unique in Christendom and reads "Here lies the body of Samuel Crooke Esq. He was kill'd going to ye Assizes by Mr William Buckley. To the Great Griefe of his family and friends August 9th 1722.

The charnel house in the churchyard of St Leonard's Church at Walton-le-Dale.

He was an Affectioned Husband and Usefull Magistrate. And a faithful subject to the best of Kings. He marry'dd Anna. Daughter of Sr. Charles Hoghton Bart. And left Issue a son Born Two months after his Death."

The church was the nearest to the home of the Houghton family, and the south chancel bears many memorials to this family, whose home still stands on a knoll above the River Darwen. The Assheton family are also remembered in the chancel, the connection probably being Cuerdale. Substantial alterations have been made to the church over the centuries, but it was necessary to prevent it falling down, and a succession of skilled architects achieved an impressive balance by retaining many ancient portions, including tower and chancel, which are incorporated into the modern centre section. The brackets for the old invasion beams have been retained. A village as old as Walton-le-Dale deserves an ancient church.

If you want to annoy a true resident then all you have to do is to refer to Walton as a suburb of Preston. He will quickly remind you of the Romans and Anglo-Saxons, the market charter of 1221, the Civil War battles and those of the Stuart risings of 1751 and 1745 for control of the crucial Walton Bridge. The saddest event at the bridge took place on 17th August, 1648, when Cromwell gave the King's men a beating which was described by John Milton, who wrote "that day Darwen ran red with blood of Scots" It is said that Cromwell stayed the night following the battle at the *Unicorn Inn*, which although reroofed remains much the same, functioning today as an Italian restaurant. The Walton-le-Dale gentry held tenaciously to the Stuarts and the Old Religion and formed themselves into what has become known as the Mock Corporation which met with great ceremony at the *Unicorn Inn*. The Corporation elected its officers, including a Mayor, although its power was extremely limited because it was obliged to meet in relative secrecy. It welcomed High Church Anglicans, who in the times following the Stuart rebellions against the Hanoverians in the eighteenth century were often suspected of Papist sympathies. Their ceremonial regalia is now kept at the Harris Museum in Preston.

Before continuing our journey along the Ribble through Preston to the sea, we should follow the river Darwen backwards from its confluence with the main river just beyond the bridge. From its source to Walton-le-Dale this is a most historic stream.

CHAPTER EIGHT

The Darwen

L IKE the Calder, this river has not been well treated and has been one of the most heavily polluted watercourses in Britain. A few years ago a retired Blackburn weaver told me, "It's still a lovely river lad—all tha's got to do is 'old thi nose". I am glad to say that things have improved a little since then.

The Darwen rises on the moors between Bolton and Darwen, at a spot called Cranberry Moss, where larks sing and curlews call. For a short distance "the cleere Darwen" is just as it was when described thus by the poet Michael Drayton (1563–1631). The landmark for miles around is Darwen Tower, a dual monument celebrating free access to all who enjoy fresh air in their lungs and also Queen Victoria's Diamond Jubilee in 1897. What a boon it must have been for hardworking Darwenites to climb up from their smoky mills and enjoy a cup of tea at the tower before ascending the stone stairs to look around the heathery moorland and enjoy the song of the birds.

The folks hereabouts have another good "lung" which can be reached more easily from the town. Sunnyhurst Wood with its café, visitors' centre and river spanned by ornamental bridges and nature trails is as lovely as its name implies. This is so especially in autumn when the colours of the fallen leaves are enhanced by a profusion of fungi including the candle snuff *Xylaria hypoxylon* and Dryad's saddle *Polyporus squamosus,* which do indeed look like tiny seats growing out of tree trunks. Dryads were tree nymphs, and the walks through the woods with tiny bridges over trickling streams do seem fairy-like, especially in the mists of an autumn morning with dew glistening on the spiders' webs. There is also a fine, labelled collection of British ferns in their own little grotto and the visitors' centre usually has an exhibition of photographs or paintings, often with a leaning towards natural history.

Just downstream is Spring Vale, a garden village built by the family of John Percival Davies, a mill owner born in 1885 and a founder member of the Fabian Society. Spring Vale garden village was a self-contained settlement on the lines of Bourneville and Port Sunlight. It was "Percy" who bought Heys Farm Guest House at West Bradford for fellow Quakers who wanted a rest from the hard world, and it was here that Gandhi stayed in the September of 1931 during his tour of the Lancashire cotton towns.

The valley must have been beautiful before the river was culverted during the construction of roads and mills as the town of Darwen slowly merged with Blackburn. Dominated by the spire of the parish church of St Mary the Virgin, which was elevated to the status of a cathedral in 1926, the old mill town of Blackburn is recovering slowly but surely from the death of King Cotton. It is fitting that the town should have grown rapidly from the village it was before the industrial revolution because James Hargreaves, inventor of the Spinning Jenny, was born in Blackburn in 1745. The growth and heyday of the cotton industry can be studied during a visit to the James Taylor Textile Museum, which contains accurately constructed working models of cotton machinery. In the days when the Lancashire towns dominated the first division of the football league I well remember sitting in the riverside grandstand at Ewood Park to watch Blackburn Rovers take on the might of Burnley, Preston North End, Blackpool and Bolton, not to mention the giants from Manchester and Liverpool. Walking to the station over bridges spanning the river, overlooked by towering chimneys and through thick fogs, was not too pleasant, but I now look forward to a stroll in the peace and quiet of nearby Witton Country Park, once the property of the Fielden family, who were intimately connected with the affairs of Blackburn for over two hundred years.

There were two branches of the family and both built fine houses along the banks of the Darwen or its tributaries. Witton House was constructed on the banks of the Blackwater (once called the Black Burn) quite close to its confluence with the Darwen. The area now occupied by Witton Park was once part of the huge Norman manor of Billington which by 1288 was in the possession of Geoffrey de Chadderton. Then it passed via the de Haldeleys, Radcliffes, Standishes and Greenfields to John Holme, who was vicar of Blackburn, and around 1742 to the Fieldens. The old hall was eventually replaced in 1800 by Henry Fielden, whose son Joseph, who died in 1870, did a great deal for Blackburn; many of its institutions owe their origins to his generosity.

There was only one blot developing on the landscape around Witton House, and that was industrial pollution, which accelerated during the period when Blackburn became a large cotton-manufacturing town. The Blackwater, which rises on the hills above Oswaldtwistle, was so badly affected that the family became very worried—they might well have been grateful for the fact that they lived almost a third of a mile from the Darwen, which was even filthier. The branch of the family living at Feniscowles and headed by Henry's brother William was obliged to vacate

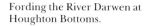

Fording the River Darwen at Houghton Bottoms.

their residence. Not surprisingly they were unable to sell it, and the house fell into disrepair and is now a rather pathetic-looking ruin.

Close by, the Darwen is joined by the River Roddlesworth, flowing down from the moors through woodland full of graceful birches where redstarts and great spotted woodpeckers breed, and ornithologists travel from miles around to watch the display flights of the tree pipits. There is a large car park and picnic site near the *Royal Arms Inn* and also a 'bus stop. A winding track follows the old stagecoach road, and you can sometimes feel the ancient stones beneath your feet. You will also find the ruins of the magnificent eighteenth-century Hollingshead Hall. A hall is mentioned here as early as 1380 and was owned by the Radcliffes of Ordsall Hall at Salford. Guy Fawkes was a relative of this branch of the family. A new hall was built by the Brock-Hollingshead family in 1776, but the area is now owned by Liverpool as a catchment area for the nearby reservoir. Close by is the "Wishing Well" which was famous for the quality of its water in medieval times; that water was considered a guaranteed cure for eye complaints. There was a small calico mill on the river but water power was never a real feature of this splendid area.

The Roddlesworth passes through Tockholes, a fine old village with terraces of old handweavers' cottages which is still an isolated spot. Even in the days when the Saxon "Toki" sought refuge in his "hollow", religion could be practised in isolation, which proved a boon in the seventeenth century when Presbyterianism was struggling to survive. Illegal coiners and distillers of spirits also found Tockholes a haven. The parish church has attractive lance-shaped windows and is reached along a narrow lane beyond the chapel. It was rebuilt in 1832. An unusual feature is an outdoor pulpit, a reminder of the days when large summer congregations could not be accommodated within. Buried in the churchyard is John Osbaldeston, who on his death in a workhouse in 1862 was described as "A Dupe of False Friends and the Victim of Misplaced

The outdoor pulpit of Tockholes Church.

Confidence". What a sad end to a genius who invented the weft-fork, which stopped the loom as soon as the thread snapped. It made a fortune for many folk—all of whom ignored John in his hour of need.

Following the Roddlesworth down from Tockholes to Feniscowles, we can return to the equally unhappy tale of the Fieldens and the polluted Darwen. In 1873 they unsuccessfully sued the Local Board of Health about the state of the river; finally in despair they moved to Scarborough. Before 1820 the waters had carried a healthy stock of both brown trout and salmon, and otter hunting was a popular pastime along the banks. The last recorded successful hunt was controlled by J. Lomax (the Lomax family came from Clayton Hall, now also sadly demolished) and made a kill just downstream at Houghton Bottoms.

Before following the same route those interested in the Darwen should divert once more into the grounds of Witton Park with its lovely woodlands, exclusive playing fields and running track and discover what happened to this branch of the Fieldens. They were generous with their "brass" and bestowed large sums of money on St Mark's Church on Buncer Lane. The family vaults are below the church and their coat of arms are above the doorway. The family have not resided hereabouts since 1947, when Blackburn Corporation purchased the estate for £62,000, assisted by a grant of £35,000 from Mr R. E. Hart, a ropemaker with an M.A. from Cambridge; he died a bachelor and left his collection of coins, books and "priceless" medieval illuminated manuscripts to the town, plus £10,000 to construct a gallery in which to keep them. The council of the 1940s was so badly organised that the manuscripts were stored and forgotten, coming to light only in 1985. The money was then worth £100,000, the gallery was built and the town now has its inheritance. What a pity the council of 1947 did not find the extra £11,000 to cure the dry rot and save Witton House from demolition. It would have made a grand museum, in every way a rival to Towneley Park in Burnley. However, the house was demolished and an excellent country park has been gradually evolved. Some of the outhouses were retained and form the basis of the visitors' centre. The lily pond and the red brick walls surrounding it are in a good state of repair and the paths through the woodlands ring to the sound of pheasants. These birds are no doubt the ancestors of those bred in the grounds when the Fieldens managed the area as a shoot.

Until 1985 the Royal Lancashire Show was held at Witton but a disagreement over rent has meant that this spectacular event has been transferred elsewhere and the atmosphere—and rent—will be sadly missed. A pleasant stroll leads close alongside Pleasington golf course and across the Darwen is the Priory of St Mary and St John the Baptist, built between 1816 and 1819 as a thanks offering by J. F. Butler. A feature of the Priory is its enormous and extremely attractive rose window. Pleasington Old Hall is a sixteenth-century house with mullioned windows, the home of John de Ainsworth, who married the heiress of the de Pleasington family.

Downstream is Houghton Bottoms, an oasis of Old England, forgotten by time and a haven for naturalists and historians alike. Many

The Methodist Chapel at Houghton Bottoms, built in 1794 and still a centre of religious life.

of the old cottages, farms and mills are now shattered ruins and even the old post office is boarded up. The old Wesleyan chapel still seems to have a strong beat and I got the feeling of a new vibrancy about the spot. A footbridge crosses the Darwen but the ford is still there and used by cattle from the adjacent farm and horses. I visited the spot during Christmas and a young lady out on her new pony was negotiating the ford, droplets

138

of water flashing up from the pony's hooves. Similar scenes must have been a local feature since Domesday.

The winding roads and paths follow the river, which although still dirty would seem to have improved since 1906 when J. T. Fielding wrote:

> What a beauty spot if only the river would promise to be sweet and clean, and not give off that offensive smell, nor gather those miniature barrels of filth for the excitement of our olfactory nerves! But it is there, and we must possess our souls in peace until the Rivers Conservancy Board has done another shuffle of the cards, and brought things to pass, which are so much desired. Amidst all our complaints, however, we glory in the presence of the trees of the forest, which so enhance the beauty of the scene, and give tone to the landscape. But there! even amidst our congratulations that the trees are still left unto us, we catch a whiff of the breeze coming from the trees themselves, informing us that their days too are numbered, and that the woodman's axe will soon do its deadly work. We hope this was a breeze that had got out of its usual course, and that some other trees were meant and not these, for what would this ravine be like if shorn of its timber? No! Woodman spare those trees! Amidst these cogitations we have made progress along the bank of the stream and now enter the defile, wherein stands the weir which was constructed to turn the water down the sluice, and so on to the mill a little further down the vale. Over the head of the weir go these lumps of putrefaction, which have accumulated for days, to be severed into hundreds of pieces on the rocks below. But what a grand gorge it is! A miniature canyon, which might have been borrowed from our friends across the Atlantic. This craggy mass has been formed by the persistent action of the river, which still goes on slowly, grinding away the rocks, and making for itself a deeper channel, whilst in the meantime rain and frost render assistance in the rending of the rocks above. We present the scene in all its picturesque beauty, after having extracted the smell, for, happily, photography has not found a means of reproducing such obnoxious fumes.

Spanning this magnificent gorge at a spot once called "owlet holes" is a tremendous railway viaduct which in the 1850s cost £10,000 to build, a not inconsiderable sum in those days, but still a bargain price. The structure soars a hundred feet above the river, supported on three sixty-foot semi-circular arches. Perhaps the cost was held down by the presence of a nearby quarry, meaning that the smooth-faced ashlar stone was available on site. The quarry is now the Mecca of local climbers who use the sheer cliffs to practise their art, and at weekends and holidays figures are seen hanging like flies beneath the tremendous and historic Houghton Tower.

The family home was established in 1266 when Sir Adam de Houghton used the site as a base for his favourite sport of hunting. It was still surrounded by rich woodlands in 1617 as King James I was touring in all his majesty through his Lancashire domains. On 15th August Sir Richard Houghton did his best to outdo all others in the extravagance of his entertainment. What a sight it must have been to see the Royal coaches drop their splendidly-attired occupants at the foot of the hill which is topped by the Tudor hall, built by Thomas Houghton in 1565.

The Sunday lunch of 19th August is remembered every day in most restaurants of the land, in particular by the dish of sirloin steak. Even the briefest of glances at the menu confronting King James puts our modern Christmas time excesses into the shade.

First Course: Pullets, boiled capon, mutton boiled, chickens boiled, shoulder of mutton roast, boiled ducks, roast loin of veal, roast haunch of venison, pasty of hot venison, roast turkey, roast swan, chicken pie hot, roast goose, cold rabbit, snipe pie, roast beef, tongue pie (cold), sprod (part) boiled, roast herons, curlew pie, mince pie (hot), custards, and roast pig.

Second Course: Hot pheasant, quails, partridge, artichoke pie, buttered peas, rabbits, ducks, plovers, red-deer pie, roast lamb, bacon, roast pigeons, wild boar pie, pear tart, turkey chicks &c, &c.

All the local nobility were present and we owe the above list to the diary of Nicholas Assheton. We can imagine the feverish activities in the kitchen as cooks and their assistants worried about the impression created by their dishes, as the young boys turning the roasting meat over the smoky fire sweated and dreamed of the rich green fields and cooling

Left: Houghton Tower, originally established in the thirteenth century as a hunting lodge.

Opposite: Lovely old stone cottages at **Houghton Bottoms.**

waters of the Darwen at Houghton Bottoms. They need not have worried because James was so impressed by his portion of loin that he raised his sword and knighted it. Here is the origin of the sirloin steaks which we enjoy to this day. For breakfast the following morning there was a dish called "umbel pie" apparently made from umbellifers—the carrot family. Some say the umbles referred to were made from the offal of deer.

The Darwen as it runs through Houghton Bottoms has changed little since the time of James I apart from being dirtier. The tree-lined valley is dominated by silver-trunked birches, some riddled with the outgrowths of fungi, especially bracket polypores, and they are an ideal habitat for the great spotted woodpecker which is resident here. In spring its rapid drumming sounds like a tiny train scuttling over the viaduct which blends surprisingly well into the scenery.

One feature which was so important in 1617 that King James insisted on paying it a visit was the alum mine at nearby Woodfold. Alum is a double salt found in a shale-like material, mainly consisting of potassium and aluminium sulphates. It was vital as a medieval styptic and for

producing mordants for fixing colours in textiles. It was also used to dress leather and size paper, and in the production of stable pigments. The King having enjoyed very expensive hospitality and hunted the local woods for boar and deer may well have wished to see one of the sources of Houghton's revenue. The mine did pay a percentage of its profits to the Crown, having been originally established by Sir Richard Houghton in the time of the first Elizabeth. It was situated close to the western border of Pleasington, near the modern golf course. The mine probably provided sufficient alum to satisfy the local area and was mentioned in Fuller's *Worthies of England*, published in 1662: "I am informed that Allume is found at Houghton in this county within the inheritance of Sir Richard Houghton, and that enough for the use of this and the neighbouring Shires though not for transportation. But because far greater plenty is afforded in Yorkshire the langer mention of this mineral". Fuller goes on to point out that Pleasington alum was in great demand by local clothiers, glovers and dyers. The mine was never to assume a high position, but was still being worked in 1771. The Blackburn parish register records the death of one John Kitchin, employed as an "Alum striker", who was buried in April, 1771.

Still in operation lower down the Darwen is a paper mill at Roach Bridge with a very impressive weir which at one time must have produced a useful head of water to drive the machinery. I visited the site in December, 1985, when the machinery was stilled over the Christmas period. Water roared over the weir and flowed under the bridge. Below I watched a grey wagtail picking about in the heap of untidy debris at the edge of the water, which although brown looked surprisingly clean and did not smell. I was just wondering if any fish lurked in these gloomy depths when my companion pointed out a kingfisher, its colours reflected in the sunlight over the water; in one subtle movement it flipped over the bridge, down through the bankside willows and was downstream in less than a couple of heartbeats.

Just upstream of this mill is Samlesbury Bottoms, which at one time was a considerable settlement. In 1784 there was a cotton mill run by William Slater with some fourteen cottages associated with it. By 1879 the cotton mill had been replaced by Isherwood's Paper Mill, and it is known that there were then twenty-seven cottages and a shop in close proximity. As we wander through the quiet solitude of these Darwen-side hamlets we must wonder what twist of fortune prevented them growing into small, or perhaps large, textile-based towns.

Onward flows the Darwen to meet the Ribble at Walton-le-Dale, a river more at peace with the world in the 1980s than it ever was a century ago but still in need of a "wash and brush up".

142

CHAPTER NINE

The Douglas

Duglesse, a riveret, creepeth and stealeth along quietly by Ormskirk, near unto which our noble Arthur, as Nennius writeth, put the Saxons to flight in a memorable battle. At the head thereof standeth the Town Wigan, called in Ancient times Wibiggin; of which name I have nothing else to say, but that in Lancashire they call buildings and houses Biggins.

This was written by William Camden (1551–1623). We can never prove if this indeed was the "Dulas" and "Duglas" of the knights of the Round Table, but there can be no doubt that the river valley was an important route both for trade and for armies. Neither can there be any doubt that Martin Mere was once a huge lake and would have served as well as any other for the disposal of the magic sword Excalibur.

The river was used as a boundary between the Saxon hundreds of West Derby and Leyland, and the name Hundred End is still used today to describe the section of the estuary just to the south-west of Hesketh Bank. In 1223 the Douglas was referred to as the Ascalon, in 1650 as the Astlan and finally in 1719 as the Asland. Asland probably referred to the host of trees including willow, alder and ash which lined its banks. In those days the Asland was thought to have two tributaries: the Yarrow (from the Celtic word for rough) and the Tawd, which is also a Celtic name in origin, meaning spreading. It is this latter tributary that today we call the Douglas. Both streams have their sources on the breezy slopes near Rivington and close to Winter Hill.

Capped by a tower built by John Andrews in 1733, Rivington Pike's 1,192-foot (363 metres) summit has been a beacon hill for centuries. Here a fire burned to celebrate the defeat of the Armada on 19th July, 1588, and walkers still seem prepared to test their heart and lungs to climb to the top. Who can blame them, for the view overlooking Lord Leverhulme's estate is said by many to be the finest in the county. I've climbed the pike many a time and I'm not prepared to contradict this statement. Before he was elevated to the peerage William Hesketh Lever had made enough money from the manufacture of soap along the banks of the Mersey to be able to purchase 2,100 acres of moorland and lay out spectacular gardens around a large wooden bungalow which he unpretentiously called Roynton Cottage! Lever never forgot the common man and much of the estate was open to the public. He must have had a lot of popular support when he strenuously objected to Liverpool Corporation's plan to construct a reservoir in the valley. On the surface Lever lost, but let us consider what he gained. He was paid twice the original purchase price, and he obtained an agreement that 400 acres were to be retained as Lever Park. Some defeat! He planted lots of trees around both the old hall and his own bungalow, which was in its own forty-five acres of gardens, set up an open-air zoo, restored two Saxon cruck barns which remain today and are unique in the North of England, and beside the tree-lined reservoir built a replica of old Liverpool Castle. I wonder if he had his tongue in his cheek when he did that.

In 1913 William was important enough to be asked to dinner with King George V and Queen Mary by the Earl of Derby. While he and his wife were enjoying themselves a militant suffragette, Edith Rigby, set fire to the bungalow and it was totally destroyed along with many valuable

Martin Mere was largely drained between 1692 and 1813, but a vestigial part of the mere is now a Wildfowl Trust reserve.

items. Within three weeks of this tragedy Mrs Lever was dead, and William's efforts were directed into rebuilding the bungalow in stone and into building his model village at Port Sunlight, which is described in my book on the River Mersey. Lord Leverhulme died himself in 1925, and his home gradually fell apart and became a hidden heap of stones beneath a tangle of vegetation. With the coming of the Country Park order was restored. The old hall, which was rebuilt in 1744, now serves as a restaurant; the church of the Holy Trinity which was rebuilt on a Saxon site by the Pilkington family in 1541 also remains, as does the old Grammar School, still in use by juniors. This was endowed by Bishop Pilkington in Tudor times.

Standing above the village is a tiny Unitarian chapel built in 1703, one of the earliest nonconformist houses in Lancashire. The box pews and the pulpit are fine examples of early eighteenth-century carving. I wonder how many of these early dissenters spent time in the stocks, which are now part of the vicar's garden furniture? Part of the old village is now under the reservoir, but enough remains to provide an atmosphere befitting an area which has been settled since the bronze age. Footpaths run throughout the area, but those wishing to trace the Douglas must journey for almost twenty-five miles through Horwich and Blackrod before turning westward from Wigan and then passing between Parbold and the Ashurst hills, and thence to Hesketh Bank and beyond it the Ribble.

Two events both due to human activities affected the flow of the Douglas. Firstly in 1692 Thomas Fleetwood, the squire of Bank Hall, worked out an ambitious plan to drain Martin Mere and use the good alluvial land so obtained for farming. A channel had to be cut to increase the drainage efficiency of the Douglas and, despite having some 2,000 men employed on the project, it proved far from easy. By 1755 the flood gates had vanished in a storm and the lake had returned. Thomas Eccleston of Scarisbrick financed a second effort around 1781 and sensibly employed the engineer Gilbert who had worked with Brindley on the Bridgewater Canal. In time the plans worked and by the late 1780s some corn was grown, although the task was not satisfactorily completed until 1813, and drainage continued until 1849. In 1961 a million-pound project involved the cutting of thirty-two miles of channel and the provision of a huge pumping system. If this system failed we should soon have Martin Mere back again with the loss of valuable farmland famous for potatoes, lettuces, celery and beetroot.

Secondly the Douglas was one of the earliest of British rivers to be converted into a "navigation". This idea of rendering rivers navigable was very much in vogue between 1720 and 1750, until canal mania took over and engineering techniques evolved that did not require a river as a starting point. As industrial and domestic demand for coal began to increase, the mines around Wigan were desperate for an access to the sea. This was provided by managing the Douglas so that small vessels could carry coal to the Ribble estuary and thence to sea. There was a big demand in Ireland and the North of Britain, including the iron smelting areas of Furness. There was even a port called Sollom built at the mouth of the Douglas during the 1730s to facilitate the export of Wigan coal. This canalisation makes the course of the old Douglas, in contrast to that of the Yarrow, rather difficult to follow. In his *History of Lancashire* of 1840 Baines tells us that:

> The Douglas, as well as the Ribble, is navigable and many small vessels from 26 to 45 tons burden, registered at the Custom house at Preston, are employed in conveying coal from Wigan to Lytham, and Preston, as well as to Ireland; and in the importation from that country of grain, meal and butter. At present there are two ferries on the Douglas, one at Longton and the other at Hoole which save a circuit of nearly four miles to Preston by the Turnpike road.

Once the Ribble's course had been altered the whole aspect of the Douglas as a working river was changed and it soon became just an industrial dumping ground. The Douglas Valley scheme has recently begun to make great improvements.

The "Bloody Mountain" of Wigan

The Douglas winds around the lands of Haigh Hall, one of ancient Wigan's most historic spots. *Haigh* is a Saxon word meaning an enclosure, and Haigh Hall is still surrounded by attractive woodlands even today. In 1188 Haigh was owned by Hugh Le Norreys but it was Mabel, the daughter of his grandson of the same name, who brought fame and perhaps a combination of fable and fact to the area. In 1295 Mabel married into the Anglo-Saxon family of de Bradshaigh. Her husband Sir William was away either on a crusade or more likely as an outlaw between 1315 and 1322. As he was missing, presumed dead, Mab married a Welsh knight—although Welsh in these days may have meant "a stranger from afar"! Sir William on his unexpected return pursued the knight and killed him at the Bloody Stone at Newton-le-Willows in 1322. Facts, however, suggest that Sir William was never a peaceful soul and he was himself killed near the Bloody Stone in 1333. Mab was apparently ordered by her confessor to walk barefoot once a week from the hall to the cross in Standishgate (removed later into the grounds of Wigan Girls' High School). She and her husband are interred and remembered in the

146

parish church of All Saints. The childless Mab was still alive in 1348 and a document of 1403 refers to Mabs Cross, by which time the lands had passed to a nephew.

They were still in the Bradshaigh family in 1651 when members of the family took part in a battle along Wigan Lane on the banks of the Douglas, in support of the future Charles II. On this occasion the King's men were routed and "the battle of the bloody mountain" was marked on many early maps. After his restoration Charles did not forget Sir Roger Bradshaigh, and the knight was made mayor of Wigan when it was given a new charter in 1660.

Apart from the great battle at "bloody mountain" Roger's energies were also concentrated on a Great Sough, a construction intended to enable him to extract coal without causing flooding or interference to adjoining lands. The project, which began tentatively in 1652, was finished, and rightly hailed as a great scientific feat, in 1670. The normal, and very unsightly, method had previously been to dig surface drainage channels. Sir Roger decided to construct an underground tunnel (the Great Sough) almost two-thirds of a mile long, six feet wide and four feet high (1.05km long, 1.8 metres wide and 1.2 metres high) draining the mines into a yellow brook close to its confluence with the Douglas. We may say that pollution began at this point. The channel was regularly inspected until 1923 when water levels reached the roof, but it is still open and functional. Haigh's was no ordinary coal, but a type called cannel, rich in volatile constituents ensuring that it burned brightly, although with some smoke. Significantly the word has the same root as candle. Although dull in its natural state, cannel is clean to the touch and will take a high polish, which made it very popular for fashioning into attractive ornaments.

When the last Sir Roger Bradshaigh died in 1770 the estate passed into the hands of ten-year-old Elizabeth Dalrymple. When she was twenty she married Alexander Lindsay, the twenty-third Earl of Crawford, who managed the estate well, even setting up an iron foundry fired by his own coal. The foundry produced castings for the famous Laxey wheel on the Isle of Man, the original purpose of which was to pump water from the 1,800-foot (584 metres) deep lead mines. Work was also carried out for the constructors of the first Mersey Tunnel. James, the twenty-fourth earl, became Baron Wigan of Haigh Hall and he replaced the ancient hall with the present structure between 1830 and 1849, although he integrated some features of the old hall. In 1947 the house and grounds were bought by Wigan Corporation and are open to the public during the summer. Nature trails lead out through attractive grounds. It is from here that strenuous and so far very successful efforts are being co-ordinated to clean up the Douglas, which over the centuries has been used and misused by the old town's most influential family at Haigh Hall.

As the Douglas curls around Parbold and Newburgh it runs close to the Leeds to Liverpool Canal, a feature which has obviously altered not only the appearance of the river but also its influence as a waterway.

Approached on an early summer's day with its gardens ablaze with colour from rhododendrons and other shrubs, the nearby Rufford Old Hall looks as pretty as the top of a chocolate box. Now owned by the National Trust (and open daily except Fridays), Rufford is a fine example of a fifteenth-century half-timbered hall. It was at one time home of the Hesketh family, which we have already met at Martholme on the Calder. The real feature of Rufford is the timber-framed hall, with one of the most magnificent hammer beam roofs in England. It is said that young William Shakespeare (or was it Shakeshaft?) acted here during a tour with a troup of actors around the halls of the North.

Time should always be spared to look at the Philip Ashcroft village museum collection in the Hall, especially, in the context of this book, at the pre-Christian dugout canoe found when Martin Mere was being drained.

The Hesketh family, despite fanatical support for the Catholic cause, managed to survive and increase to such an extent that Rufford became too small for their needs and they moved in Georgian times to a more suitable dwelling on the opposite side of the present A59 Liverpool road. This building now serves as a hospital.

In the early days the hall must have been close to the shores of Martin Mere, which would have provided the kitchens with a wealth of wildfowl. The drainage of the mere has reduced the wildfowl considerably but since the 1970s the Wildfowl Trust has established a refuge consisting of 385 acres of invaluable marsh and pools. There is a collection of wildfowl from all around the world, visited by many children, and the centre has a well-deserved reputation for educational excellence. It is also a good spot for a family day out. It is, however, not a zoo since the bulk of the area is left wild; from the hides species such as ruff, short-eared owls, hen harriers, whooper swans and a host of wildfowl can be seen. The flock of up to 20,000 pink footed geese are a truly magnificent sight, not to mention the almost deafening sound as they came in to roost.

At Bretherton the River Yarrow joins the Douglas after rising close

A stone-paved street leads to the church of St Michael and All Angels at Croston.

to the latter on the fells around Rivington. It skirts neatly around Chorley and Birkacre before slicing through the lovely old village of Croston, one of the most attractive spots associated with the Ribble and its tributaries. Birkacre is a nature reserve in a valley formed by the Yarrow; it is run by the county council mainly for the use of schools. Chorley forms the eastern barrier, while away to the west is Coppul. The area was a vaccary (cow farm) way back in 1250 when the Lord of Charnock gave it to his sister, probably as a wedding present. There is further documentary evidence that in 1398 John de Coppull allowed Robert de Burgh to use the power of the Yarrow to drive a grain mill. In 1423 on the death of Robert the lands were divided between his three daughters, one of whom constructed a Walke Mill, which was used for washing cloth. The lack of documents would suggest a period of peace, but in the 1770s all this was to change; living at Birkacre House was one Richard Arkwright, whose spinning mill was too efficient for the local folk. On 9th October, 1779, an account tells us:

> In the neighbourhood of Chorley the mob destroyed and burnt engines and buildings erected by Mr Arkwright at great expense. Two thousand upwards attacked a large building near the same place on Sunday (Oct 8th) from which two rioters were killed and eight wounded and taken prisoner. They returned strongly enforced on Monday and destroyed a great number of buildings with a vast quantity of machinery for the spinning of cotton. Sir George Saville arrived with three companies of York Militia while the buildings were in flames. The rioters sometimes spared spinning jennies with twenty spindles or fewer since these could be worked by hand, but destroyed all those driven by horse or water power.

The works were eventually rebuilt but were never prosperous, mostly concentrating upon printing, dying and bleaching under a number of owners. In 1876 the firm McNaughton and Thom, calico printers, took over. Thom became known as an excellent chemist; he worked out how to extract paraffin from shale. Thom died in 1899 and two years later Birkacre was used by his sons as a factory for bleaching, a process which continued until the depression of the 1930s. This must have caused heavy pollution to add to that due to coal mining further up the valley, an enterprise in which John Thom was also involved. Almost all remains of the works have gone. Wigan Angling Club has stocked the mill ponds with fish and nature is swamping the valley in a curtain of greenery. Giant horsetails grow by the waterside; so rough are they that they were once used as pan scrubbers. The horsetails are related to the ferns but have both fertile and sterile fronds serving as landing areas for dragonflies and damselflies which abound at Birkacre along with diving beetles, water boatmen and a host of flowers and birds. Lovely growths of reed mace provide perching spots for blue, great and coal tits.

Onward runs the Yarrow to the little village with the big church: Croston, which was indeed an ancient town with a cross. My first introduction to Croston was while making a series of programmes for BBC Radio Lancashire on village churches. St Michael and All Angels is a mighty big church, with records going back to 1094, which once served all the surrounding villages including Chorley, Rufford, Tarleton, and Bretherston. Parishioners must have found the way to church a real nuisance at times when the Yarrow was in flood and they had to journey through deep mud and often take to rowing boats. During the draining of Martin Mere and other low-lying areas the water table was lowered, but Croston was regularly flooded until the 1940s. Much of this old marshland is now converted into arable fields.

I stood on the little hump-backed bridge built in 1682 at a cost of £30 and looked up the Yarrow to the church on its banks, its peal of bells

The packhorse bridge over the River Yarrow at Croston.

ringing out over the valley as the campanologists practised their art. I made my way past a huddle of quaint old cottages facing a cobbled road leading to the church. The entrance is guarded by an ancient and modern cross—the base is Saxon while the shaft is a replacement made in 1953 from an old millstone. At the church gates I met Bob Bretherton, one of the churchwardens, who showed me the almshouses built close to the church by the Reverend Streynsham Master in 1802 to commemorate the Jubilee of George III. The Master family have had a long and continuing rectorship at Croston, but none lived longer in body or in folklore than Streynsham, who died in his ninety-eighth year. His advice to his people in times of flood was "Clay up the front door and put the pigs in the house." He actually provided a savings bank for the villagers in 1818—there were not too many such institutions about in those days. He richly deserved his name of King Croston. The churchwarden showed me the lovely white-painted rectory and took me around the church, pointing out many of its treasures. He pointed out the double piscina in the south wall which has been dated between 1250 and 1350 and which was sealed up at the Reformation, to be discovered during the

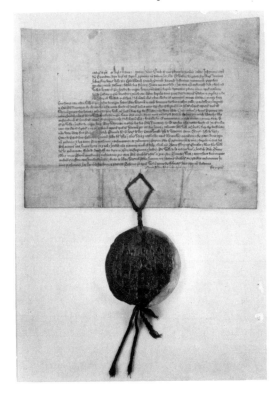

Croston's charter.

Almshouses at Croston, built in 1802 to commemorate the Jubilee of King George III.

restoration of the church in 1866. Before the Reformation there were three chantry chapels in which poorly paid priests said masses for their founders, in this case John Todd, the Chaplain at Rufford (1500), Christopher Walton (before 1527) and Catherine Tarleton (1530). There may well have been a fourth called the Becconsall Chantry chapel in the churchyard, probably on the site of a schoolroom. This was first established in 1372 by John of Gaunt and salvaged by James Hiet in 1660. The tower bears the arms of the Hesketh family, since Croston was the nearest church to their lovely old hall at Rufford.

No sooner had the bells ceased ringing than I could hear the sound of the Croston Morris Dancers at practice. Only re-established in recent years, the dancing troupe is already well known in the county and does its own village proud on Coffee Day. The origin of this day is not known but it takes place during July and the village lets its hair down. Gaily decorated horses pull floats, there is a procession of witness along the street to the church and a fun fair is held in the garden of the Georgian rectory. In 1983 the village celebrated the 700th anniversary of its charter, confirmed by Edward I and allowing Croston a weekly market and an annual fair.

From Tarleton to the Ribble

Just after its confluence with the Yarrow the Douglas meanders through the old settlement of Tarleton where the manorial courts were held at the *Ram's Head Inn*, the present building dating back to 1640 when it was a farmhouse. Drivers from Preston to Southport know well the infamous Tarleton twin bridges which cross the Leeds and Liverpool Canal and the Douglas, and are a well-known accident black spot. Close by is the Church of St Mary, built in 1719 to replace an earlier church which was closer to the Lord of the Manor than to the village itself, then situated at the end of a rutted cart track. Although they still had to use the old church for burials the villagers did finally get their own church in the 1880s. Near the modern road is the fascinating Bank Hall House, now part of the Lilford estates. The one-time home of the Banastres, the Fleetwoods, including Thomas the drainage engineer, and the Leighs of Lyme, the house was rebuilt in 1808, a fascinating feature being a tower with stone carvings showing chess pieces.

Further downstream on the way to Much Hoole is the lovely old Carr House which is not so much a curiosity but a house of world-wide reputation for the role it played in astronomy. To discover its secret we must pay a visit to Westminster Abbey and seek out a tablet which reads:

> In memory of Jeremiah Horrocks, Curate of Hoole, in Lancashire, who died on the 30th January 1641, in or near his 22nd year; Having in so short a life Detected the long inequality in the mean motion of Jupiter and Saturn; Discovered the orbit of the moon to be an ellipse; Determined the motion of the lunar apse; Suggested the physical causes of the revolution; And predicted from his own observations the Transit of Venus, which was seen by himself and his friend William Crabtree on Sunday 24th November, 1639. This tablet, facing the Monument of Newton, was raised after the lapse of more than two centuries. December 9th, 1874.

The house associated with this young genius is close to the junction of Carr House Lane, which was on the old Turnpike road, to which we will return later. Carr House was built by the Stones brothers, Thomas and Andrew, for their brother John. An inscription over the door reads "Thomas Stones of London, haberdasher, and Andrew Stones of Amsterdam, merchant, hath builded this house of their own charges and giveth the same to their brother John Stones Ano Domini 1613". It is not known whether John was a poor sheep farmer down on his luck or a rich sheep farmer providing wool for the family export business, but whatever its origins the house is a fine example of Jacobean architecture. It was constructed of hand-made bricks and had mullioned windows and leaded panes. Carr House was almost lost to us until restored and used as Barry Elder's Doll Museum, but has been privately owned since the latter moved to Lancaster. As a student in London I noticed the memorial to Jeremiah Horrocks, and discovering where he was from I referred to Herbert C. Collins' book *Lancashire Plain and Seaboard*, published in 1953, and absorbed every word as he took his readers on a memorable journey.

From Tarleton to Preston the modern highway plays hide and seek with the Old Turnpike Highway. Turn off down any of its curving narrow lanes and you will be rewarded with old Lancashire villages, old inns and forgotten smithies, even a turnpike milestone hidden in the overgrown hedgerows. Having crossed the river Douglas and the canal it is not long before the road from Bretherton comes in; on the right stands Carr House to which I will return in its proper place. Just now we will follow the old Turnpike by bearing left and coming to Much Hoole church, which has been isolated from the village by the later arterial road. I found the door locked so I could not see the three decker pulpit (1695) but the exterior is quaint and unusual.

Much Hoole was constructed in 1628 as a chapel of ease to Croston, and at that time Jeremiah Horrocks was nine years old. He had been born in what was then the village of Toxteth outside Liverpool and went to Emmanuel College, Cambridge, but failed to graduate, preferring to concentrate on astronomy. He was appointed curate at St Michael's Church, Much Hoole, and added to his meagre income by tutoring John Stones' children, lodging in a room over the porch. He calculated that on 24th November, 1639, the planet Venus would pass between the earth and sun, a transit never previously witnessed. He and his friend William Crabtree of Broughton, near Manchester, waited eagerly but were almost disappointed. Let Herbert Collins complete the story

. . . an autumn mist obscured the sky. Then at a quarter past three in the afternoon the mist suddenly cleared, the sun shone out, and he saw the new spot, of unusual size and perfectly round, on the left of the sun. Astronomer Crabtree in Manchester was also watching by prior arrangement. They each projected the sun's image through a telescope on to a piece of white paper in a darkened room with identical results. The calculations had been checked by Gascoyne, inventor of the micrometer.

What a pity that one with such obvious talent should die so young. He is commemorated in a stained glass window and a mural tablet in the chancel at Much Hoole as well as the tablet in Westminster Abbey which fired my curiosity almost thirty years ago.

Just before the Douglas empties into the Ribble it flows close to Becconsall and Hesketh Bank, which modern travellers often view as an uninteresting cul de sac, unless they happen to be naturalists intent on watching the birds of the marshland. Before the river was canalised the coach road led across the marshes, but most signs of this have now disappeared beneath the salt marsh vegetation. The route of the old coach road crossed first the Douglas and then the Ribble, ending at the Guide House at Freckleton. The crossing was fraught with danger and in the churchyard at Becconsall is buried James Blundell, who drowned while misjudging the tide on 6th July, 1844. On his tombstone is the following verse:

> Often times I have crossed the sands,
> And through the Ribble Deep.
> But I was found in Astland drowned
> Which caused me here to sleep.
> It was God's will it should be so,
> Some other way we all must go.

CHAPTER TEN

Preston to the Sea

THE town of Preston came into being because it guarded a vital crossing of the river, while beyond it the Ribble flowed wide and strong to its estuary.

The settlement at Walton-le-Dale is an ancient one, but precisely when Preston itself originated has been difficult to establish. It does, however, seem likely that it was indeed a Priests' Town, the clerics concerned apparently coming from the monastery at Ripon. The Ribble crossing between Preston and Penwortham would have been particularly important in the sixth and seventh centuries since the river was the border between the ancient Kingdoms of Mercia to the south and northern Northumbria with its power base in Yorkshire.

The discovery of the Cuerdale Hoard has already established that the Saxons and Vikings were active around Preston, and the area can seldom have been peaceful, with much ebbing, flowing and mixing of populations taking place. Celts, Scandinavians and Angles were all present, judging by local place names, the Norwegian influence being particularly strong with names such as Hesketh, Savick and Salwick indicating a direct connection with the latter culture. I have read histories suggesting that lack of direct evidence relating to Preston's importance before the eleventh century means that no substantial settlement existed. This must be doubted because the first mention of Preston lists it as the most important town in Amounderness, which included the land between the Ribble and the River Cocker, embracing both the Fylde and the Forest of Bowland. An important town can hardly have sprung up overnight, and it is far more sensible to assume that early records have been lost. Judging by the visits medieval Preston received from the invading Scots, this would be hardly surprising.

Preston was on the old road which ran through Warrington (where a vital bridge spanned the Mersey) and Wigan before continuing via Cockersand to Lancaster and thence to Kendal, Carlisle and Scotland. Add to this the presence of a developing port and we have the seed of a vital trading settlement. Trade attracts people and Preston soon had a thriving market, confirmed by the Royal Charter given by Henry II in 1179, the earliest such grant in the area.

In view of this it is perhaps surprising that a stone castle was never constructed at Preston. It seems reasonable to suppose that if an enterprising Norman had built his pile overlooking the Ribble then Lancaster would not have become the dominant influence in early Lancashire. Trade was regulated by a Guild of Merchants, which some folk think dates back to Saxon times. Locals have a saying that a rare event takes place "Every Preston Guild". Since 1562 the Guild ceremony has been held at intervals of around twenty years. Nowadays it is purely a pageant, but what was the Guild in its early years? Residents of the old town were allowed to trade freely, but were obliged to stick to agreed prices and practices and were governed by their Reeve, who was equivalent to a modern mayor or chairperson of the council. Regular meetings called portmotes were held and anyone wishing to trade free from tolls in Preston had to plead his case before the court. The Guild was certainly a useful thing to belong to and functioned rather like an insurance company. The merchants certainly needed financial protection since plague was one problem and rapacious Scots were another worry, not to mention civil wars especially between the Roses of Lancaster and York and then the Stuarts' confrontation with Parliament.

In modern Britain with our freezers, tinned and convenience foods, we tend to forget how vital good harvests can be until our attention is drawn to the pathetic state of African countries in the grip of drought and crop failure. Medieval Britain had just this problem and the Preston district had three disastrous harvests between 1314 and 1316. Recovery was slow and things had not returned to normal when Preston was devastated by the army of Robert the Bruce on his infamous 1322 "tour of northern England." A report of 1341 noted a great deal of distress and poverty still apparent in the town following the Scots' raid, and in 1347 came the first visit of the dreaded Black Death, during which 3,000 people died, a substantial proportion of the population. The plague returned in 1361, 1369 and 1630.

Although Tudor Preston was important there was little urban development beyond the main streets of Churchgate, Fishergate and Friargate. The latter refers to a tiny Franciscan priory which was in use in 1221 but never seems to have had any real influence over the area. This probably accounts for the fact that Preston did not become embroiled in the Pilgrimage of Grace, which as we have seen was so disastrous along much of Ribblesdale. Preston folk were, however, slow to abandon the

St Warburg's Church at Preston, seen across the Ribble from Penwortham.

old religion, although Protestants and Catholics initially lived at peace as the market town became prosperous. As Tudor England settled down to a period of peace new industries including woollen weaving and flax weaving brought Preston both fame and good wages. By the time James I passed through Preston in 1617 on his way to Houghton Tower there were three markets each week, on Wednesdays, Fridays and Saturdays. Then came the plague; it has been suggested that at the end of 1630 there were only 887 people left alive in the town, and 756 of these were in need of financial aid. Next came the Civil War; it is hardly surprising that Preston folk wished to be left alone during this period, but Preston's strategic importance was far too great for that to happen.

The thunder of war echoed around Preston rather than exploding within it, but the town remained loyal to the King. In February, 1643, the Parliamentarians approached from Manchester and a bloody encounter resulted. The valiant Royalist Adam Morte lived up to his name by being killed. The victorious Roundheads led by Captain Booth did not hold Preston for long and in March the Earl of Derby restored the town to the King, only to have to give it up again when the war was lost. But the real battle of Preston was yet to come, as Sir Marmaduke Langdale and the Scot George Munro marched down from Scotland in an attempt to restore Charles I to his throne. The 17th August, 1648, was the most crucial day in the life – and death – of Charles I. Before Preston there had been an armed truce and Charles could well have negotiated for, and been granted, an honourable peace. After Preston there was no way back. As far as Cromwell was concerned the King had broken his word and re-opened hostilities. He must now be tried for treason and die. Both Charles and Cromwell knew this as their armies manoeuvred around the fields to the east of Preston.

On paper the Royalists ought to have won easily as they had 20,000 troops against fewer than 9,000 Roundheads. Winning battles, however, depends as much upon organised staff work and imaginative leadership as upon mere numbers, and in these departments the Royalists' Duke of Hamilton and the Earl of Callendar were no match for Oliver Cromwell and John Lambert. Although the battle on the surrounding moors was a bloody affair the main engagement left the town undamaged and in the main fiercely loyal to the Stuart King's cause. The restoration of Charles II in 1660 was greeted with something akin to hysteria. When James II tried unsuccessfully to restore the old religion and was replaced by the Protestant Hanoverians, Preston was not pleased and Preston men were ready to welcome the 1715 Stuart army marching south from Scotland. The second battle of Preston did involve some street fighting; although the rebels did well they soon realised there was no general support for

The Harris Library and Museum, part of Preston's rich heritage of nineteenth and early twentieth-century buildings.

their cause further south and retreated. While they were there the gallant gentlemen seem to have had other things on their mind besides fighting, and a contemporary account stated that "The Ladys in this toune, Preston, are so beautiful and richly attired, that the Gentlemen Soldiers minded nothing but courting and feasting." I wonder how many of Bonnie Prince Charlie's army of 1745 could remember the ladies of

161

Preston when they returned to an attractive town with such mixed memories. After the rebellions of 1715 and 1745 Preston continued to attract influential gentlemen and ladies of fashion, a combination which created what became known as Proud Preston. One of its main social occasions was the by then ceremonial Guild.

Soon, however, the Preston of history and elegance was to give way to the Preston of the industrial revolution, and King Cotton won the battle for the town which King Charles had so tragically lost. Industry

Preston Docks, seen from across the Ribble. The mv *Manxman* is now permanently moored in the docks and used as a night club.

demanded better roads, and then the Lancaster Canal opened in 1789. In 1803 a connection was made to a branch of the Leeds and Liverpool Canal at Walton summit via a horse-drawn tramroad. Later steam took over from horses. This should be regarded as an early example of a railway with an increasing importance as industry gathered pace and demanded a reliable delivery of coal to power its boilers and a transport system to carry the manufactured goods away. Flax and hemp weaving were the first industries, the former being imported from Ireland through the quays developing along the Ribble. Richard Arkwright was born in Preston and while living in Stoneygate in 1768 he invented the spinning frame which allowed cotton to be spun mechanically. John Horrocks, who initially employed teams of hand loom weavers, built his huge mills, and gas lighting allowed shifts of operatives to work around the clock. Preston's place in industry was assured and its history was swamped under a mass of back-to-back and terraced houses.

It was during this period that some of the finest buildings in Lancashire were constructed in Preston. It was a pity, however, that much of medieval Preston was destroyed at the same time. During the Guild of 1882 the foundation stone of the Harris Library and Museum was laid, the building being completed in 1903. The Market Square at last had neo-Greek buildings around it which were thought to be in keeping with the town's fine history. The nearby sessions house, designed by Henry Little in the English Baroque style, was completed at the same time. Banks, a railway station and the Town Hall sprang up along Fishergate.

I have heard it said that the Victorians and Edwardians destroyed Preston's history. We would be far better off not crying over spilt milk and looking upon the town as a priceless example of late nineteenth and early twentieth century architecture. Preston should remember that in 1815, the year of Waterloo, it was the first provincial town to be lit by gas.

After almost a century of prosperity Preston's textile industry, along with that of the rest of Lancashire, went into decline and the docks no longer buzz with activity. As a frequent visitor to Preston rather than a resident I have two memories of the town; one of them is of the once-busy docks, the other of a tradition that still thrives. My father once took me to Avenham Park to join the throngs of Easter revellers enjoying the ritual of "pace-egging". Groups of young in body and young in heart made their way to the grassy slopes of the park above the Ribble, carrying baskets of hard-boiled eggs stained and brightly painted. Pairs of "eggers" rolled their attractive prizes towards each other, the owner of the undamaged egg being the winner. In the end hard-boiled eggs form the basis of a picnic. All the revellers ask for is a fine day, which is more often than not denied them, but it takes more than a drop of rain to stop these folk from enjoying themselves.

I am rather more sad when I think about the docks. In the 1950s I was allowed aboard a vessel bringing timber into Preston Docks and travelled with her as she inched her way up the straight, canalised river on high tide to her berth, surrounded by towering cranes. The smell of diesel and sea water was diluted by the resinous smell of wood. After nervously walking down the gangplank into the busy heart of dockland I was taken to a first division football match at Deepdale to watch Stanley Matthews of Blackpool match his skills with those of Finney of Preston. All was well with the world and I thought that nothing would ever change at the end of a perfect day.

As I write today Preston and Blackpool languish in the third and fourth divisions and the docks are being demolished with the decline of trade, as Britain looks towards Europe rather than America and west coast ports becoming uneconomic. Although landing areas were present in the fourteenth century and were more important than those at Liverpool in the sixteenth century, the main efforts to widen the navigational channel and keep it dredged did not begin in earnest until the latter half of the nineteenth century. While the docks were being constructed the axeheads and arrows of Neolithic man as well as an ancient canoe were discovered, along with the bones of beasts such as giant deer and other long extinct animals. The antlers of red deer were also unearthed. The dockland complex now being demolished was only built in the 1890s and had an effective working life of less than a century. An integral part of the old dockland was Thomas Ward's shipbreaking yard which broke up old vessels including the White Star liner *Adriatic*, whose 3,888 tons had carried her 900 passengers plus crew across the Atlantic in record time soon after her launch in 1872. By 1899 her time had come and she sailed for the last time up the Ribble to be broken up. Many of her fittings were incorporated into what became known as the Adriatic Dance Hall in Preston. Strangely enough a similar event has recently taken place. The old Isle of Man ferry *Manxman* is now the lone occupant of Preston's dockland, having been converted – not without considerable teething troubles – into a floating nightclub. While writing this book during the cold winter of 1986 I had cause to drive past the dock on a dark wet evening. There was *Manxman* lit up as workmen restoring her came to the end of their shift. The darkness hid the devastation of dockland and all I could see was this lovely old ship reflected in the cold clear water, and memories came flooding back. After a brief look at the Ribble's most important town the time has come to follow the course of the river alongside its southerly bank to Southport.

Via Penwortham to the coast

A historian friend of mine once remarked with only part of his tongue in his cheek "If you want to follow the history of Preston go to Penwortham." On reflection I am sure he was right, because archaeological evidence compiled in the last century proves that a Roman road ran from Penwortham to Walton-le-Dale, a logical path although two fords existed across to the bank on which modern Preston now stands. Much of Penwortham's history lies beneath modern buildings befitting a settlement now mainly used as Preston's dormitory. I was once returning from Southport to Preston along the A59 and as I chatted to a friend about the traffic jam he quoted Hewitson, who travelled the same route in the nineteenth century and wrote "We passed gaily through Penwortham with its wealth of foliage . . . A very old place indeed is Penwortham

Penwortham Church. There has been a church on the site since Saxon times.

and it probably possesses finer and more historic associations than any other country place contiguous to Preston."

The reason for its importance lies in its strategic position set on a rock above a ford of the Ribble. The name derives from *pen* meaning a hill, *weid*, a ford, and *ham*, a settlement. There was certainly a Saxon castle on the hill, and before 1066 the lands belonged to Edward the Confessor. William gave all the land 'twixt Mersey and Furness to his kinsman Roger de Poicteau, who had fought valiantly at Hastings. This turbulent Norman constructed a motte and bailey castle on the Saxon site and sub-let his vast estates so that Warin Bussel held Penwortham. When Warin's son Roger married into a family living in Evesham, a group of monks from the Benedictine Abbey there were given leave to establish a small priory at Penwortham. This was begun in 1075 and dissolved in 1535, the building and associated land and grange being purchased by the Fleetwood family for a princely sum of £3,088. When we think of the value of money in those days it is no wonder that Henry's exchequer benefited from the demise of the abbeys.

When Margery Fleetwood married Lawrence Rawstorne in 1660 a link was forged with the Croston family. In 1832 another Lawrence Rawstorne built a grand house on the site of the old priory. What a pity that this was demolished in the 1920s when a group of houses was constructed along the lane leading up to the magnificent church dedicated to St Mary. The present building is basically fifteenth century but the chancel is early fourteenth and some alterations were carried out at various times in the nineteenth century. There has been a church on the site from at least A.D. 644, obviously associated with the Saxon settlement protected by the castle on the hill overlooking the ford.

In 1798 a map drawn up by Robert Porter shows two fords, the wide, comparatively shallow course of the river being split into two branches by an island called the Holme, but the original course is not now apparent because of alterations made during the construction of Preston Docks in 1892. When did Penwortham get its own bridge? A ferry had operated up to 1755 when a bridge was constructed, but within a year the bridge fell into the river. It was replaced in 1759 and still stands, although the modern road bypasses it.

After Penwortham comes Hutton which provides us surprisingly with the most important piece of Penwortham's history. During road construction in 1928 the castellated priory lodge was moved, stone by stone, into Hutton. It makes a lovely-looking cottage and so well does it fit into the local scene that few realise just how much out of context it is. Before exploring Hutton time should be spent looking at Howick Cross. A glance at the map will reveal the extent of the marshlands around the tidal Ribble. These are dominated by plants such as thrift, sea aster, sea plantain and sea purslane and echo to the sound of wading birds such as redshank and curlew. The little villages on the higher, drier banks must have been very isolated and subject to frequent flooding. Only the works concerned with producing a Ribble channel suitable for large ships to run up to Preston Docks removed the main dangers. Visitors to Howick Cross are often confused by the fact that there were two fine old houses here known as Howick Hall and Howick House. The hall is the older of the two, becoming a farmhouse at the turn of the seventeenth century when William Norris built a "New Hall" (now called Howick House) in a style which is basically Elizabethan but can often lead to the belief that the building is older than it is. After being owned for a while by the Rawstornes it passed into the hands of the Shuttleworths, whose coat of arms can be seen above the lodge. The twenty-one-acre garden was famed throughout the country in the 1870s for the aroma of its roses, the succulence of its strawberries and the variety of the plants grown in a heated greenhouse. The horticultural tradition was maintained by the paper-making family of Wrigley who took over from the Shuttleworths, and during the 1890s the gardens were famous for the dazzling array of azalias. After a period of military use during the 1939–45 war the house became the Galloway Home for the Blind in 1951. Just beyond it, close to the crossroads, is Howick Free School, which functioned from 1727 and 1828. The base of the old cross can also be seen here.

During my early teens my father was a keen crown green bowler and on a couple of occasions I accompanied him to play in matches at Hutton, the headquarters of the Lancashire Police, and was always given time to explore the village. Hutton Hall was demolished in the 1930s but some idea of the extent of its grounds can be appreciated by visitors to the police training school which stands on the site.

Lawrence Hutton Rawstorne, who was born at Hutton in 1744, set Lancashire's agriculture firmly on the national map with the publication in 1843 of his classic *Lancashire Farming . . . with some suggestions for remedying defects*. This tradition is carried on to this day by the nearby Lancashire College of Agriculture. It is possible to wander around the county and see trees and shrubs laid out to provide cover for game. The plans for such areas were probably copied from Rawstorne's *Gamonia or the Art of Preserving Game and an Improved Method of Making Plantations and Covers*.

Hutton Grammar School is an attractive boarding school which had its origins in Longton as a chantry funded by William Walton in 1517, the Grammar School being endowed by William's nephew Christopher in 1552. In 1746 the school moved to Hutton, where it was rebuilt in 1826;

at first all the village children were taught free. By 1882 the present format was in being and an advertisement in the Preston Guild Programme for that year boasts that the school, which charged thirty-nine guineas per year, "occupied a very healthy situation about a mile from the West Lancashire Railway which is being constructed from Preston to Southport". It was forcibly pointed out that each boy had a bed of his own, a real luxury in the context of the age. In 1931 other accommodation was provided. As with many similar institutions, girls are now an important part of the sixth form scene.

The modern traveller along the banks of the Ribble could be excused for asking the precise location of the river. In the old days the river was wide and shallow, but as ships increased in size during the industrial revolution the channel was deepened to form what almost constituted a canal. The old fishing ports were thus left high and dry. Here we stand

Spartina colonising an estuarial mudflat. This vigorous plant has colonised the Ribble between Southport and Lytham and is helping to hasten silting of the river.   *John Clegg*

today among the old docklands and riverside inns which have retained much of their atmosphere, despite having lost their tidal river.

On we go downstream. Despite a new bypass the old ribbon villages of Longton and Hoole on the old road take us to the junction with the Douglas, described in Chapter Nine. Longton village struggles along for four miles, but even now is not more than a mile wide. Once on the old turnpike road with its ancient inns the feeling of old Longton can be gained by following footpaths to such places as Old Grange Farm. It lies on the edge of the old Ribble channel but is now protected by a high dyke. I remember as a child the excitement of standing below this dyke and watching the masts of ships travelling up to Preston Docks, looking as if they were sailing through fields of yellow buttercups. Later in life I listened to the sound of wintering birds, but if a real ornithological treat is required we must travel to the marshes at the mouth of the Ribble.

The Nature Conservancy Council's National Nature Reserve can be reached by following the path via Old Hollow Farm. The reserve, so important for wintering geese and wildfowl, has not been without its share of controversy. Since 1979 when sanctuary areas were set up the wildfowl counts have risen, but wildfowling is still allowed on the reserve. This has not pleased a number of local residents and naturalists who go to watch birds and instead find them dead and dying on the tideline. Shooting has been recently restricted, and it is to be hoped that with the pressure off the pink-footed geese will exceed their 1986 levels of 15,000 and the wigeon numbers may go above 18,000. Teal, pintail, shelduck, mallard, redshanks, curlews and bar-tailed godwits are also features of the reserve.

There is also good birdwatching along the shore road into Southport when whooper and Bewick swans are among the wintering birds, while birds of prey such as short-eared owls and hen harriers hunt the waders in the salt marshes. The neck of the river between Southport and Lytham is being restricted by silting due to the lack of traffic upriver, but this process is being accelerated by the presence of rice grass *Spartina x townsendii*. This vigorous plant is actually a hybrid between the European species *Spartina maritima* and the American cord grass *Spartina alterniflora* which arrived by accident in Southampton Water in 1870. At first it was heralded as a magic plant which stabilised mud and increased the speed of development of salt marshes, allowing more stock, particularly sheep, to be grazed. To seaside resorts, however, the loss of their vital sand has proved to be alarming, to say the least. Both Southport and Lytham have cause to worry, but before concluding this book with an account of the two resorts let us return to Preston and briefly follow the north bank of the Ribble.

The North Bank and the sea

Until the opening of the M55 the A583 was heavy with summer traffic on its way to Blackpool and the Fylde coast. Few could spare the time to look towards the canalised river surrounded by the ancient marshes of Lea and Clifton which once provided wildfowlers with good catches to take to the markets at Kirkham and Preston. Those veteran travellers in the know would take the A584 just before Clifton and travel to Blackpool via Lytham. Before the modernisation of the sewage works at Freckleton this was one of my favourite birdwatching haunts.

A minor road and footpath leads towards Naze Mount, from where it appears to be a reasonable risk to cross the river. Not so! It was a skilled job to guide people safely across the channel, the safest point actually being from Warton, beyond the present airfield complex. In 1870 trained guides were still meeting the train at Wrea Green and leading nervous travellers from Warton across the Ribble to Hesketh, with the daunting prospect of a second struggle across the Douglas.

The lovely old *Ship Inn* at Freckleton looks every inch a haunt for smugglers, as indeed it was, and in the days before Preston Docks demanded the canalising of the Ribble, Freckleton built her own wooden ships. Seagoing vessels anchored to transfer their cargoes to shallow-draught barges for transfer upstream to Preston. At Warton the marshlands, which for thousands of years echoed to the exciting notes of wintering wildfowl, have in the last fifty years also heard the roaring of aircraft from the British Aircraft Corporation factory. Americans were based here during the war, and a tragic event happened when one of their bombers crashed on Freckleton school causing much loss of life. After the war the Tornado aircraft was partly constructed at Warton, as were sections of the graceful but noisy Concorde. To recognise this fact the supersonic airliner was once flown at minimum speed and minimum height down the Ribble; according to locals its noise caused local babies, dogs and cats to set up a concerted howl!

In the County Record Office in Preston are wartime German photographs of the marshland airfields. I wonder if the reconnaissance pilots were interested in the airfields or had got wind of the well-kept secret—it is still not well known—that a prototype of the mulberry harbour used in the invasion of Normandy was built and tested at Lytham. At that time Lytham had a shipbuilding tradition spread over sixty years during which eighty ships, mainly tugs and ferries, had been fashioned by the bands of "sand grown 'uns" as Lythamers were called. The Lytham-built steam launch *Zaire* operated for many years on African rivers and was used in the film *Sanders of the River*. The last ship to be built

A fishing boat at its moorings in Lytham Creek.

was the *Windermere Ferry*, but small boats are still built and repaired in the historic yard.

Lytham St Annes is usually listed as a seaside resort, but this does not do justice either to Lytham, which is an estuary town with a shipbuilding tradition, or to St. Annes, which was a bathing resort and a product of nineteenth-century improvements in transportation, particularly the railways. In the context of this book only Lytham should be considered as it guards the estuary of the Ribble along with Southport on the opposite bank. Lytham may be said to begin at Saltcotes, a name which clearly indicates its value as a producer of salt, a vital commodity since civilisation began.

Initially Lytham was built on the edge of a salt marsh, probably around the Benedictine priory constructed as a cell of Durham Abbey, but no direct remains can be found today. There was, however a

171

The wreck of the *Mexico* lying on the Southport shore after the 1886 lifeboat disaster which cost the lives of twenty-eight lifeboatmen.

settlement called Lethum in existence before the Conquest. After the dissolution of the abbeys in the 1530s the priory came into the possession of the Clifton family, who had been influential in the area since at least 1258. It does seem certain that the Cliftons' Lytham Hall built in 1625 was constructed using material from the priory, but the massive reconstruction supervised for the family between 1751 and 1764 by John Carr of York removed much of the evidence, although some historians feel they can recognise the odd religious stone here and there.

The whole area was dominated by the Clifton family, who suffered greatly for their strict refusal to compromise their Catholic views. They were descended from the Norman Osbert Lord of Salwick and in an isolated land bounded by the Ribble and Wyre rivers they were allowed to act as virtual monarchs. Cliftons led their men into battle against the Scots, Welsh and Irish as well as in France where they fought valiantly at Agincourt. Throughout this time the Cliftons were ardent Catholics, and as the country turned towards Protestantism, the family reputation began to suffer. At first they avoided penalties but in the Civil War they suffered along with the King, who was convinced he ruled by Divine Right. Some of the young men of the family perished by the sword, another was an active Jesuit priest and yet another perished in Manchester gaol following his capture near York after fighting with Prince Rupert. Thomas Clifton survived the war, but Parliament exacted a high price in fines; although his son, also named Thomas, was in favour with the newly restored Charles II he was given no money. Thomas was no doubt delighted with being created a baronet, but one suspects that what he really needed was cash! Sir Thomas was not lucky in his family life either, seven of his children, including his male heir, dying before their father. In 1694 when William III was being hard pressed by the combined opposition of the Tories, the Jacobites, the Catholics and for a while the Whigs too, the frail old Sir Thomas was dragged off by Dutch mercenary soldiers to face charges of "Papist conspiracy" in Manchester; he died soon after his return.

There can be no doubt that the gentry and the country folk thought alike in the early days of the Reformation in their desire to hold tight to the old religion. By the time of the 1715 and 1745 rebellions, however, the local peasants had put up with being "cannon fodder" for quite long enough and relationships with their masters became increasingly uneasy. They were probably much more in agreement with the re-designing of Lytham Hall and also the work-generating schemes to drain the marshes and create both pasture and arable land. Lytham Hall is no longer a private residence, but a nursing home. Building in the vicinity has certainly gone on apace, but the lovely old green is still dominated by its splendid white-painted windmill, constructed in 1805 on a site which might have had a mill upon it since the twelfth century. I have frequently seen the mill from the sea when easing my way on the flood tide in a small boat into the Ribble estuary. This can be a treacherous coastline and was the scene of a great tragedy in British lifeboat history. On 10th December, 1886, the German owned barque *Mexico* was being battered by a storm and lifeboats were launched from Lytham St Anne's and Southport. The whole fourteen of the Lytham St Anne's crew perished, and of the Southport crew of sixteen only two survived. A memorial can be seen in the Alpine gardens, and as usual it took tragedy to focus attention on a problem. Great improvements were made in lifeboat design following the Lytham wreck.

At the mouth of the river on the opposite bank stands the old village of Churchtown. Beyond it is the area known as South and North Hawes. There was a church overlooking its own little town in 1178, dedicated to St Cuthbert. Many historians believe that in A.D. 687 the bones and associated relics of Saint Cuthbert were carried around the county to keep them away from the Danes; his bones rested in twelve places, including Heysham, Lytham and Mele, which was the old name for Churchtown. As early as 1219 on the Sunday following 20th August (St Cuthbert's Eve) the tradition of "Bathing Sunday" had become established. Churchtown also had a reputation for providing accommodation for travellers awaiting suitable low tide conditions in which to cross the channel to Lytham. Thus Churchtown had a tradition of bathing and accommodation—all that was needed was to combine these two and we have an early example of a holiday resort. The enterprising gentleman to do this was an innkeeper at Churchtown by the name of William Sutton. Although he overstretched his limited financial resources by 1803 and was imprisoned for debt, he had already established his place in the history of our seaside resorts. He set up bathing machines and a teashop to the south of Churchtown and ran a horse and cart shuttle service to what soon became known as his South Port and a little later became known as Duke's Folly. Still later his judgment was proved to be sound. Southport went from strength to strength as visitors poured in, including thousands from the developing coalfields around Wigan and the cotton towns of East Lancashire. Day trippers from Wigan travelled along the Leeds and Liverpool Canal, a branch of which opened in 1774, and which went through Scarisbrick, a mere four miles from Southport. With the opening of the railway in 1848 the steady flow of visitors became a deluge and the future of the resort dominating the Ribble estuary was assured. The American Nathaniel Hawthorne, who lived in Southport between 1856 and 1857, described the scene thus:

> It is a large village, or rather more than a village, which seems to be almost entirely made up of lodging houses, and, at any rate, has been built by the influx of summer visitors; a sandy soil, level, and laid out with well paved streets, the principal of which are laid out with bazaars, markets, shops, hotels of various degrees, and a showy vivacity of aspect. There are a great many donkey carriages—large vehicles drawn by a pair of donkeys; bath-chairs with invalid ladies; refreshment rooms in great numbers—a place where everybody seems to be a transitory guest, nobody at home.

The heyday of the British seaside resorts disappeared with the coming of efficient and cheap air routes bringing the more reliable sunspots of Europe within range of working families.

As I came to the end of my journey down the Ribble the sun was beating down from a blue sky, the high tide was lapping against the promenade as if to refute the comedians' jokes about the sea at Southport. A small, gaily painted boat bobbed on the water at the entrance to the river and the seaside gardens were ablaze with flowers. Little has changed since Victorian times but the river, as with many

Lord Street, Southport, early in the twentieth century, with an electric tramway running along the highway.

others, has a lesson for us mortals. However we misuse our watercourses, nature can, and will, recover. Once a working river with much of the pollution associated with industry, the Ribble, with just a little help from its friends, is recovering. There are now fewer black spots and, as I hope this book has shown, many beauty spots along its length. It has taken us from the heights of Ribblehead, through water meadows and a series of cotton towns, and down a man-made channel to the glorious estuary where sea breezes blow and birds abound.

175

Bibliography

Ackerley, Rev. F. G. *History of Mitton*, Aberdeen University Press, 1947.
Aspin, C. *Lancashire, the First Industrial Society*, Helmshore Local History Society, 1969.

Bagley, J. J. *Lancashire*, Batsford, 1972.
Bailey, F. *A History of Southport*, Angus Downie, 1955.
Baines *History of Lancashire*, Preston, 1836.
Barron, James. *History of Ribble Navigation*, Guardian Press, 1938.
Blackburn Directory (1818).

Carr, R. *English Fox Hunting: a History*, Weidenfeld and Nicolson, 1976.
Catlow, Richard. *Ribble Valley Rendezvous*, Countryside, 1979.
Cotterall, John. *North Meols to South Ribble*, Neil Richardson, 1985.
Cowpe, F. *Walton-le-Dale—a History of the Village*, Guardian Press, 1954.

Dobson, W. *Rambles by the Ribble*, Simpkin Marshall & Co., 1881.

Edwards, B. J. N. & Webster, P. V., editors. *Ribchester Excavations Part 1*, Cardiff University, 1985.
Elgee, F. & W. *Archaeology of Yorkshire*, S.R. Publishers, 1933.
Eyre, Kathleen. *The Real Lancashire*, Dalesman Books, 1983.

Fishwick, Henry. *A History of Lancashire*, Elliot Stock, 1894.
Freethy, Ron. *Exploring Pendle*, Countryside, 1983.
Freethy, Ron. *Exploring Villages*, Countryside, 1985.
Freethy, Ron. *The River Mersey*, Terence Dalton, 1985.
Freethy, Ron. *Wakes Seaside Resorts*, Faust, 1986.
Freethy, Ron. *Northern Abbeys*, Countryside, 1986.
Freethy, Ron. *The Natural History of Rivers*, Terence Dalton, 1986.

Hallum, J. *The Surviving Past*, Countryside, 1985.
Harrison, S. W. *A History of Penwortham*, Curriculum Development Centre, Preston, 1983.
Higham, M. C. *Slaidburn: a Brief Guide for Visitors*, privately printed booklet, 1985.
Hodge, A. C. and Ridge, J. F. *Ribchester: a Short History and Guide*, Carnegie Press, 1984.
Holmes, R. *The Battle of Preston, 1648*, Mercia Publications, 1985.
Horrocks, J. *Observations of the Transit of Venus*, Gaythorpe, 1639.
Houghton, A. T. R. *The Ribble Salmon Fisheries: Materials for a History*, Chetham Society, 1945.

Langshaw, A. *A Guide to Clitheroe Castle*, Kaydee; Clitheroe, 1947.
Langshaw, A. *Clitheroe's Thousand Years*, Borough Printing Co. Ltd., 1956.
Leigh, Val and Podmore, Brian. *Outstanding Churches in Craven*, Bradford Diocesan Board of Finance, 1985.
Lofthouse, J. *Three Rivers*, Robert Hale, 1946.
Lofthouse, J. *Lancashire Countrygoer*, Robert Hale, 1962.
Lofthouse, J. *Portrait of Lancashire*, Robert Hale, 1967.

McKnight, H. *Shell Book of Inland Waterways*, David and Charles, 1975.

Mill, David. *Place Names of Lancashire*, Batsford, 1976.

Millward, R. *Lancashire* (Making of the English Landscape Series), Hodder and Stoughton, 1955.

Mitchell, F. S. *The Birds of Lancashire*, Gurney and Jackson, 1892.

Mitchell, W. R. *Exploring the Ribble Valley*, Dalesman Books, 1979.

Oakes, C. *The Birds of Lancashire*, Oliver and Boyd, 1953.

Palmer, W. T. *Wanderings in Ribblesdale*, Skeffington, 1951.

Perkins, J. A. *History of Tarleton and Hesketh Bank*, Perkins, 1982.

Spencer, K. G. *The Status and Distribution of Birds in Lancashire*, K. G. Spencer, 1974.

Williams, E. *Walks and Talks with Fellman*, Ainsworth, 1951.

Maps

Ordnance Survey 98 2cm to 1 km Wensleydale and Upper Wharfedale

Ordnance Survey 103 2cm to 1 km Blackburn and Burnley

Ordnance Survey 102 2 cm to 1 km Preston, Blackpool and surrounding area

A rural scene on the River Dunsop at Dunsop Bridge.

Index

Illustrations in bold type